fun Ideas for the family-friendly church

Group
Loveland, Colorado

Fun Ideas for the Family-Friendly Church

Copyright © 2000 Group Publishing, Inc.

Visit our Web site: **www.grouppublishing.com**

Credits
Contributing Writers: Michael D. Warden, Jim Kochenburger, E. Paul Allen, Brian K. Burchfield, Ann Calkins, Tim Kurth, Lana Jo McLaughlin, Curtis Rittenour, and Michael W. Sciarra
Editor: Michael D. Warden
Creative Development Editor: Jim Kochenburger
Contributing Editor: John Fanella
Chief Creative Officer: Joani Schultz
Copy Editor: Betty Taylor
Art Director: Kari K. Monson
Cover Art Director: Jeff A. Storm
Cover Designer: Andrea Boven
Computer Graphic Artists: Pat Miller and Tracy K. Donaldson
Illustrator: Dick Daniels
Cover Photographer: Craig DeMartino
Production Manager: Alexander Jorgensen

Library of Congress Cataloging-in-Publication Data
Fun ideas for the family friendly church.
    p. cm.
  ISBN 0-7644-2160-3
  1. Church work with families. I. Group Publishing.

BV4438 .F86 2000
259'.1--dc21
                                                    99-089658

10 9 8 7 6 5 4 3 2 1   09 08 07 06 05 04 03 02 01 00

Printed in the United States of America.

Contents

Service Projects 59

Relationship Builders 81

Introduction

Does this scene sound familiar to you?

A family drives to church. Upon arrival, they grunt or nod at one another, then split off according to age or gender. Dad goes to the men's study group while Mom heads for the nursery, where she works as a volunteer. The teenage son strolls toward the youth building for his weekly "Hour of Power" while the two younger siblings go to "Kids' Club."

For years, this weekly breakup has been called "family ministry." Churches have prided themselves on offering a wide variety of "family ministry" programs and services, such as marriage retreats, parenting classes, youth service projects, and backyard Bible clubs for kids. Of course, these ideas are not bad. In fact, they're great! But they all operate under the same assumption: that the best way to serve families is to break them up into their respective "satellite" groups. Preschoolers go here, elementary kids over there, and youth way, way off over there. This approach can (and has) been effective at helping families. But it isn't always the best way. And, thankfully, it isn't the only game in town—not anymore.

Welcome to the new paradigm of family ministry! This new approach to family ministry is based on a simple but profound truth: There is power in letting families learn and grow together—*as families*. What would happen if you taught a Sunday school class that incorporated and involved every member of the family, a Sunday school in which families learned and studied and discussed things together? Churches that have tried this approach report that their families are growing closer, learning more, and getting stronger in their faith—just by doing things together at church. Consequently, more and more churches offer family-friendly events in which family members learn, worship, and serve together.

That's exactly why this book was created. In *Fun Ideas for the Family-Friendly Church,* you'll find *learning activities* to help family members explore the world around them and see how that world connects with God's Word, *worship experiences* that help families learn how to worship God together, *service projects* that challenge and equip family members to serve God and others, and *relationship-building activities* to draw family members closer to one another and to God. *Fun*

Ideas for the Family-Friendly Church gives you the tools you need to help families grow spiritually together as *families* and not just as individuals who happen to ride to church together.

Here are some tips to help you use the ideas in this book more effectively:

• **If you don't already have an organized family ministry program in your church, start one.** You may not be able to hire a family minister or allocate large sums of money to family ministry, but that doesn't mean family ministry is out of reach. All you need is monthly "family night" at the church and this book. Once you use the ideas in these pages, you'll soon discover a strong family ministry taking shape right before your eyes.

• **Don't keep all the fun to yourself.** Instead of trying to plan and lead all of these events yourself, invite specific families to take the lead in preparing some of these activities for the rest of the families in your church. Remember: Effective family ministry encourages *families* to do things together. So don't be afraid to let families lead families.

• **Make room for every type of family you have.** Not all families look alike, especially these days. In your church, you most likely have some single-parent families, some blended families, some extended families, some families with adopted children, and some families with no children at all. You'll also have some families with older teenagers and others with kids in preschool. Feel free to adapt the activities in this book to fit your particular mix of families. (In most cases, you can do this simply by modifying the discussion questions to fit the dominant age-level of your group.) And in those few cases where the activity is aimed at a particular age group, we say so—right in the "Family Focus."

• **Don't single out the singles.** If you have singles in your congregation, there's no reason why you can't include them in these family activities. Rather than relegating the singles to their own group (like "Friends"), encourage families to "adopt" one or more singles, then invite the singles to join in on the family festivities. Not only will the singles feel more a part of the congregation, but your families will also be enriched by the experience.

• **Every now and then, use these activities to replace your regular Sunday school or Sunday evening schedule.** Holding monthly "family nights" is a great idea. But it isn't the only way to use these activities. Every so often, shake up your regular schedule by having families meet together for Sunday school (or your Sunday evening worship time) so you can lead them through one of these activities. Doing this will help families see your commitment to family ministry and will enable them to get to know one another more effectively.

So, go ahead. Dive in to the ideas, and pick one or two you'd like to do soon. Once you get started, you'll soon create a family-friendly environment in your church that will help family members grow closer to one another and to God.

Learning Activities

Stars in Your Eyes

Category: Learning Activity

Time: 1 to 2 hours

Family Focus: Families will join you for a special "Star Night!" in which you'll introduce three easy guides to the night sky and will invite everyone to go outside to enjoy stargazing.

Supplies: You'll need black construction paper, pencils, copies of the "Stargazer Illustrations" (p. 11), and a light source (a wide-lens flashlight works well). Tell anyone who owns binoculars to bring them for scanning the sky.

Invite your guests to join you on a unique adventure, away from computer and television screens and other digital equipment, to enjoy God's "wide-screen wonder"—the night sky!

Before going outside to stargaze, explain that it would be helpful to get to know three easy "sky guides" to help you find your way in the night sky: the Big Dipper, Polaris (the North Star), and Cassiopeia. Show pictures of these three from a star chart or beginner's astronomy book such as *Exploring the Night Sky* by Terence Dickinson (Firefly Books).

Give each person one sheet of black construction paper and a sharpened pencil.

Also give each person a copy of the "Stargazer Illustrations" (p. 11) of the Big Dipper, Polaris (the North Star), and Cassiopeia. Have participants use their pencils to punch out star designs in the construction paper that match the illustrations. Tell participants to place the Big Dipper on the bottom left of the page, the North Star at the top middle, and Cassiopeia on the right.

Family-friendly Advice

Because winter skies provide the brightest star viewing, you might wish to schedule this family activity just before Christmas. Be sure to check your local weather forecast for a cloudless night sky.

When everyone has finished punching out their star designs, darken the room and use the flashlights behind each black paper to illumine the star design. Then turn on the lights, and ask everyone to join with his or her family to go outside. Distribute binoculars so that each family has at least one pair. Remind stargazers that it won't be difficult to find these three star shapes because they are among the brightest in the night sky.

When families are ready, give these instructions: **In winter, look to the northeast for the Big Dipper. Its seven stars are easily distinguishable in a "potlike" shape.** Tell children: **Stretch out your fingers to see if the Big Dipper is as wide as your outstretched hand. (It is!)**

Now find the star on the outermost lip of the Big Dipper (from which you would "pour" if it were a real pot). Put the thumb of your left hand at that spot, and stretch your fingers out wide. Just a short space past your little finger, you'll find Polaris the North Star.

The North Star is not the brightest star in the night sky—it ranks 36th in brightness if you are looking at stars from Canada or the United States. But it's very special because it is almost exactly above the North Pole of the earth. If you face the North Star, you will look due north.

Now look for the constellation Cassiopeia. It is easy to find because it consists of five stars in the shape of the letter W. Can you find it near the Big Dipper?

If you're an adventurous stargazer, use your binoculars to scan sections of the night sky. Check out the craters on the moon, the rings of the planet Saturn, and groups of beautiful star clusters. You won't be disappointed!

After the stargazing experience, have families gather together and read

Psalm 19:1-2 and Psalm 8:3-4. Then ask:

- **How does it make you feel to look up at the night sky?**
- **How do you think the heavens "display knowledge" night after night?**
- **What does the night sky tell you about the glory of God?**

Have families read Philippians 2:14-16a. Then ask:

- **How does it feel to be compared to a star shining in the night?**
- **Why does God want you to shine like a star?**
- **This week in your family, what's one way you can "shine like a star"?**

After families have discussed the last question, close your time together by having participants tell each member of their family one way he or she has been a "shining star" in their lives.

Taking It Home

Encourage families to visit their local library during the week and note names of constellations or star patterns that they can identify from their homes at night. Also encourage them to tell one another whenever anyone in the family has a "shining star" moment.

Taboo Terminology

Category: Learning Activity

Time: 1 to 2 hours

Family Focus: Families will practice talking about Jesus with others in a way that non-Christians can understand.

Supplies: You'll need copies of the "Taboo Terminology" box (p. 12), Bibles, paper, crayons or markers, pens, a candle, and a lighter.

As families arrive, give them each a "Taboo Terminology" handout (p. 12). Within their family, instruct members to each take one minute to describe how they came to know Jesus, or the difference God has made in

Stargazer Illustrations

North Star •

•   •   Big Dipper

Cassiopeia

their lives. Before families begin, say: **There is one catch to this activity. You may not use any of the words on the "Taboo Terminology" handout. Each family will start the activity with 100 points. Each time a family member uses one of the "Taboo Terminology" words, your family will lose a point.**

When everyone has understood the rules, have families begin the activity. After everyone has shared and all points have been subtracted, have families discuss these questions:

• **What was your family score?**

• **How did you feel during this activity? Why?**

• **How satisfied were you with your ability to talk about your relationship with God without using "Christianese" terminology?**

• **How was this experience like trying to talk about Christ with someone who isn't a Christian?**

• **Why is it important to talk about Jesus with others in a way they will easily understand?**

Distribute paper, crayons or markers (for children), and pens (for adults). Have each family member divide his or her paper into four equal rectangles to begin to create a "personal faith story" page. In each of the rectangles, have family members each write one of the following headings: "How I met Jesus," "What Jesus has done for me in the past," "What Jesus does for me now," and "Why I want other people to know Jesus." Have family members each write brief responses to the headings in

Taboo Terminology

You can't use these words or phrases during your one-minute talk:

conversion, convert, or converted	saved
salvation	(under) the blood, blood-washed, or
born again	blood-bought
baptized	gospel
anointed	asking Jesus into my heart
confirmation	Spirit-filled
repent or repentance	received (or accepted) Christ

each rectangle—without using the words on the "Taboo Terminology" handout.

When participants have finished, have them set their faith stories aside, and open their Bibles to 1 Peter 3:15. Before anyone reads the passage, light a candle and turn off the lights. Holding the candle, walk as far away from everyone as possible, and turn around so your back is toward the group. Have family members try to read the Bible passage. (If the room is dark enough and you are far enough away, no one should be

family-friendly Advice

If you use this activity in the daytime, tape dark plastic or paper over the windows to make the room as dark as possible for the candlelight portion of this activity.

able to read anything.) Now slowly turn around, and walk toward the group. Have family members raise their hands when they can read the verse. Ask one or two volunteers to read the verse aloud.

Blow out your candle, turn on the lights, and say: **Just as you couldn't read from the Bible because you had no light, non-Christians can't understand how to know Jesus unless someone tells them. And when we do tell them, we must share our stories without using "religious" words. Of course, the most important way to communicate our relationship with Jesus to others is through our actions.**

Read aloud Matthew 5:14-16. Ask:

• **In what ways has your "light" been hidden from the non-Christians around you?**

• **What can you do to make your light shine more brightly?**

Have participants share with their families what they wrote on their personal faith story pages. Invite family members to offer suggestions on how each person can make his or her faith story even clearer. After each person has shared, close by having family members pray for one another that each family member's light will shine brightly and clearly in the world.

Taking It Home

Encourage families to get involved in activities within their communities that will help them form friendships with more non-Christians. Challenge families to deepen their understanding of people who have a different (or no) faith and to learn how to share their faith in Christ in simple, respectful ways.

Family Ties

Category: Learning Activity

Time: 2 to 3 hours

Family Focus: Families will participate in a series of activities that emphasize the importance of family unity.

Supplies: For each family, you'll need a Bible, twenty feet of rope, poster board, markers, and masking tape. For the "Family Glob Race," you'll need to tape a start line at one end of your room. For the "Family Gopher Chase," you'll need to make several copies of the "Gopher" handout (p. 17). Post the gophers in different places around the room.

Clear all furniture from the middle of the room. As families arrive, give each a rope. Explain that families will work together to conquer several challenges involving rope.

As families complete each challenge, encourage them to discuss these questions:
- **How did it feel to work as a team with your family in this activity?**
- **What did this challenge teach you about family unity and cooperation?**
- **How can you apply what you've learned in this activity to your family life?**

Here are the challenges:

Family Circle

Family-Friendly Advice

To make the challenges easier, have smaller families combine for these activities so that each group has at least four people.

Have family members sit on the floor in a circle, with their feet touching in the center of the circle. Have a volunteer in each group tie one end of the rope around his or her waist. Then pass the rope around the circle. As each person gets the rope, have him or her wrap it once around his or her waist, then pass it on to the next person. When the rope has gone full circle, have the initial volunteer tie the rope to the ring around his or her waist, making sure the rope is pulled tight around the circle. On "go," have family members join hands and try to stand together, without allowing their hands or arms to touch the floor.

Family Glob Race

Have family members form a tight huddle behind the start line. Then wrap the rope around them and tie it off. On "go," have families race to touch the far wall of the room and then return to the start line.

Family Gopher Chase

With the rope still around them (as in the "Family Glob Race"), have families race to touch all the gopher pictures posted in the room. The first family to touch all gopher pictures wins. To make this even more fun, have volunteers move the gopher pictures from place to place after the race begins.

Family Rope Spell

Families should untie their ropes, then find a clear space on the floor. On "go," have families compete to be the first to spell each of the following words using their rope: team, love, bond, ties, close, trust, honor, bless, right, peace.

After families have conquered all the challenges, gather everyone together and ask:

• **How do you feel about your family unity? Explain.**

• **What lessons did you learn about family unity through these challenges?**

• **What are some ways you can apply what you've learned to everyday life in your home?**

Read Romans 12:9-19, then ask:

• **What's your reaction to this passage?**

• **How can this passage serve as a recipe for building family unity?**

• **In what ways does your family or other families you know do a good job staying close-knit and united?**

• **Why do you think your family (or another family) is so good at this?**

Give each family a sheet of poster board, then ask one member of each family to write this unfinished statement: "To promote unity and cooperation in our family we must…" Have families work together to brainstorm as many endings to the unfinished statement as possible. After several minutes, have families share some of their ideas with the group. Then have family members join hands and pray that they'll be drawn closer as a family and will learn to live in unity with one another.

Taking It Home

Have families take home their posters. Encourage each family to display its poster where everyone can see it. Challenge family members to add ideas to the poster during the next few weeks.

....

All Creatures Great and Small

Category: Learning Activity

Time: 3 to 4 hours

Family Focus: Families with young children will enjoy an event that focuses on the great and wonderful creatures God has created.

Supplies: For each person, you'll need a name tag with an animal's name written on it. You'll also need a Bible; room decorations with a "wild animal" or "jungle" motif; a storybook on animals, such as *James Herriot's Treasury for Children* (St. Martin's Press), or *All Creatures Great and Small* by James Herriot (St. Martin's Press); and a meal consisting of burgers, potato chips, and lemonade.

You'll need to advertise this event beforehand so families will come prepared for the day's events. Ask children to come dressed in animal costumes or to bring their favorite stuffed toy animals. Decorate the room with animal posters and any other items that highlight animals. Have the food prepared so that it will be ready to eat about twenty-five minutes after families have arrived.

As each person enters the room, stick the name of an animal on his or her back. Don't let them see the names of the animals. Tell participants to guess which animals are on their backs by asking others only "yes" or "no" questions.

When families are ready, gather everyone in a corner of the room and invite them to sit on the floor. Then ask costumed children to take turns sharing which animals they are dressed up as, and what they like most about those animals. Or

Gopher

If you don't have a zoo in your city, you can create a "pretend" zoo in your church by setting up "cages" and asking adult volunteers to dress up as specific zoo animals. As kids explore each "cage," have the "animal" talk about its life (where it lives, what it likes to eat, and so on). At each station, have the animal give kids a treat that represents the kind of food the animal eats. For example, a monkey could hand out bananas, a squirrel could give away nuts, and a lion could give samples of beef jerky.

ask children to simply show others their favorite stuffed toy animals.

Next have someone read a story about an animal, something fun for the whole family. The short stories in *James Herriot's Treasury for Children* (mentioned on page 16) are excellent. After the reading, invite a few people to each share one thing they've learned about animals from the story.

After the story time, invite everyone to enjoy a meal that includes foods with animal names. For example, Pink Flamingo Juice for pink lemonade, Lion Burgers for hamburgers, or Chimpanzee Chips for potato chips.

After the meal, have families carpool to the local zoo, where they can take kids on an adventure to discover some of the wonderful creatures God has made.

Halfway through the zoo visit, gather everyone at a central location to listen to two short Bible stories about animals. Read aloud Genesis 1:20-25—the story of the creation of animals. Also read the story of Noah and the ark, especially the mention of animals in Genesis 7:1-5 and 8:1, 15-21. Then have families continue their adventure.

At the end of your adventure, gather everyone together and pray, thanking God for the beautiful creatures he's made for us to enjoy. Invite everyone to give thanks for a specific animal he or she has enjoyed.

If you have time after your zoo adventure, you might also watch a short video (thirty minutes) on animals. There are lots of options available at your local video store or library, or for purchase. Here are a few suggestions:

• National Geographic's *Really Wild Animals* series, ASIN: 6304586027

• BBC's *All Creatures Great and Small* series on the life of British veterinarian James Herriot, ASIN: 6304972938

• Moody Institute of Science's *The Wonders of God's Creation: Animal Kingdom,* (www.moodyvideo.org)

• Integrity Music's Just for Kids, *Barnyard Fun With Duncan and the Donut Repair Club,* featuring Rob Evans (www.donutman.net)

Taking It Home

During the coming week, encourage families to continue reading stories about animals from age-appropriate books. Children can enjoy making books by cutting pictures of animals from old magazines (like National Geographic) and pasting them onto blank pages as parents read.

Out on the Wild Frontier

Category: Learning Activity

Time: 2 to 3 hours

Family Focus: Families will search for food, facts, fun things, faces, and flags from foreign places!

Supplies: For each group, you'll need a copy of a missions information book such as *Operation World* by Patrick Johnstone or a world atlas, a flashlight, a pen or pencil, slips of paper, and a fact sheet. For each country you examine, you'll need a copy of that country's flag, labeled with the name of the country on the back; a photograph of a person from that country; and a few index cards that each contain one "fun trivia" item about that country that isn't included on the fact sheet.

This event requires a little extra preparation, but it's well worth the effort. Select several countries that are known to persecute Christians, or countries that have little or no Christian presence. For each country, you'll need to create the following items:

• Fact sheet—a page that lists questions about the country, such as these: How many people live in this country? How many Christians presently live in this country? What is the main religion in this country? What kinds of food do the people eat? What kind of money do they use? What languages do they speak? (The same fact sheet can usually be used for all the countries.)

• Answers to the fact sheet—slips of paper that each contains an answer to

Family-Friendly Advice

If you have the space, you might consider expanding this activity by hiding the scavenger hunt items in various places all around the church building.

one of the questions on the fact sheet.

You may want to recruit a children's Sunday school class to make the flags and other volunteers to find the answers to the fact sheet questions and to collect the other supplies you'll need.

When you have all the supplies, hide things in various places around the room. Then turn off all the lights.

As families arrive, have them form as many groups as you have countries to assign. When people are in groups, give each group a flashlight, pen or pencil, and a fact sheet. Assign a country to each group, then explain that groups will search (in the dark) throughout the room, hunting for their assigned countrys' four F's: facts (fact sheet answers), faces (photograph of a native), fun trivia (there may be more than one), and flags.

Assign a certain number of points for each item they find. If teams find a clue or anything else from a country that belongs to another team, they must leave it where they've found it.

At a predetermined time, have everyone come back together. Then discuss these questions:

• **What was the most fun aspect of this experience?**

• **What was the most difficult thing about the experience?**

• **What is the most interesting thing you've learned about your country?**

Have group members take turns teaching the rest of the group what they've learned about their country. Then have teams come forward so you can see who's found the most things and who's earned the most points. Congratulate the winning team.

Have each group read Matthew 5:14-16 and 1 Peter 2:9-10. Then have groups discuss these questions:

• **How is the darkness we experienced in our search like the darkness non-Christians experience in life?**

• **How can we shine the light of the gospel in spiritually dark places?**

• **Do you know any people from the country you searched for? If so, do they know about Jesus?**

• **How can your family share Jesus with the people of these countries this week?**

Planting Seeds

Category: Learning Activity

Time: 60 to 90 minutes

Family Focus: Families will receive a packet of seeds to plant.

Supplies: For each family, you'll need Bibles, a packet of flower seeds, potting soil, plastic cups or small clay pots, paint, paintbrushes, glitter, beads, and glue.

Before the event, set out the supplies on tables. As families arrive, have them gather their supplies and sit together at a table. Have each family group read Mark 4:1-9. When families finish, say: **This story has a lot to say about seeds and soil. In this parable Jesus talks about seeds that fall on hard ground at the side of the road, seeds that fall on rocky ground, seeds that fall among thorns, and seeds that fall on good soil. As Jesus points out, our hearts can be a lot like soil. At various times in our lives, our hearts might be hard, rocky, or full of thorns. But what we really want is for our hearts to be like the "good soil"—open to receive God and what he has to say.**

Have families discuss these questions among themselves:

• **What makes your heart hard toward God?**

• **What usually makes your heart "soft" toward God?**

• **How does the Bible help your heart to be soft and open to God?**

Have family members work as a team to decorate their clay pot or cup. Be sure they include their family name somewhere on the pot. When they've finished, have them discuss these questions:

• Why do people decorate pots and other types of containers?

• How is decorating the outside of a pot (or cup) like trying to make ourselves look good to others "on the outside"?

• Is it wrong to try to make ourselves look good to others? Why or why not?

Have families fill their clay pots with dirt. Then ask:

• Why should we focus on what's "inside" our hearts and not just our outward appearance?

Say: One reason we should focus on our hearts is simply because our hearts provide the "soil" for God's seeds of abundant life. Without good soil, his seed will never take root in our lives.

Have families plant their seeds in the clay pots. Then ask families to read 1 Corinthians 3:6-9 and discuss the answers to these questions:

• How can we keep our "soil" ready to receive God's Word?

• If you could ask God for any kind of "seed" to be planted in your heart, what would you ask for? For example, would you ask for patience, the ability to love someone, or something else? Explain.

• How can you "plant" seeds of truth in your life and in your family?

When families have finished, have them look at their clay pots. Say: You may not see anything right now, but we know the seed has been planted. It will sprout and grow. The same process works in our hearts as well. In your life, you may not see everything you want to see. But God has seeds that can transform us into his image. And if we remain open to him, and walk in his ways, new life will come out of our hearts.

In a closing prayer, have families praise God for specific ways he helps them grow and then ask for help in the areas they need to grow.

Taking It Home

Have families take their pots home. Encourage families to care for their seeds by watering them often and by giving them lots of sunshine. When the plant begins to sprout, have family members gather together and share positive ways they see God's "seeds" of truth taking root in their own lives.

Butterfly Transformations

Category: Learning Activity

Time: 40 to 60 minutes

Family Focus: Families will learn about butterfly transformations and compare that process with God's redemption.

Supplies: For each person, you'll need a copy of the "Butterfly Designs" handout (p. 26) and two wire coat hangers. For each family you'll need a Bible, a supply of construction paper, colored markers, scissors, tissue paper, tape, (or spool of pliable wire), wire cutters, and glue.

Give each person a copy of the "Butterfly Designs" handout (p. 26) and two wire coat hangers (or a spool of pliable wire for each family). Give each family a supply of construction paper, colored markers, scissors, tissue paper, tape, wire cutters, and glue. Using these supplies, have each person create a butterfly. If they want, let participants use the "Butterfly Designs" handout as a model for creating their butterflies. But encourage participants to make their butterflies as unique as possible—something that reflects their own personalities.

While they're working on their creations, lead the following discussion. Provide the answer to each question only after allowing several people to respond:

• **Who can guess how many different kinds of butterflies there are in the United States and Canada combined?** (750 recorded.)

• **What do you think is the wingspan of the largest moth in the world?** (The Atlas moth of India has a wingspan of ten inches, tip to tip.)

• **Who can guess the wingspan of the Golden Pygmy (hint: think small)?** (One-fifth of an inch.)

• **Why do you think God made so many different kinds of butterflies?**

When participants have finished with their butterflies, have them share their creations with their families. Encourage participants to each tell their families how their butterfly creation is (or isn't) like them. After families have shared, hand out pens or pencils and have each person refer to his or her "Butterfly Designs" handout. Point out that the handout is divided into three sections: "Caterpillar Stage," "Pupal Stage," and "Butterfly Stage."

Briefly describe each section by saying: **The caterpillar stage is that time in a butterfly's life when it doesn't have any wings and it isn't very pretty. All it does during this stage is lay around and eat. It's storing up energy it will need in the future.**

The pupal stage is a "hidden" time in a butterfly's life, when it seals itself off from the rest of the world and undergoes a fantastic transformation. During this time, the caterpillar is actually totally re-created into something completely new. Butterflies in the pupal stage may even look dead to an observer, but amazing changes are taking place.

Finally, the time comes when the insect is ready to emerge from the pupa. Once it breaks out of its shell, the butterfly's wings are all wrinkled and wet. But, after just a few hours, they dry out, and the butterfly is ready to ride the winds. The transformation is complete.

Ask families if they have any questions about the transformation process, then say: **On your handouts, put your initials under the heading that corresponds to the stage of life you think you are in right now. For example, are you a caterpillar—maybe not all that beautiful, nor ready to fly, but digesting everything around you to prepare for your future? Or are you in the pupal stage—hidden from the view of most people, with seemingly nothing much going on, but you know God is making deep changes in your heart? Or are you a butterfly—ready and willing to soar the heights, having left behind an old life that now seems like a distant dream?**

Have participants share their answers with their families and explain why they answered as they did. Then have families read together 2 Corinthians 5:17-19 and discuss these questions:

- **Does God really change lives? Why or why not?**
- **Has God significantly changed your life? Why or why not?**
- **What changes would you still like to see in your life?**

Under the "Caterpillar Stage" heading, have participants write one or two qualities they have that they'd like God to change. For example, a person may have a problem with anger or may be unable to get organized. Then under the "Butterfly Stage" heading, have participants write one or two ways God has transformed their lives. When participants are ready, have them share their responses with their families.

When families have finished, say: **In closing, I have one more assignment for you. Under the "Pupal Stage" heading on your handout, write an honest prayer to God, asking him to do the work necessary to transform you completely from a caterpillar to a butterfly.**

When participants have finished, close the activity by having family members take turns reading their prayers to their families.

Taking It Home

Have participants take their butterfly creations home and hang them where they will see them often. Encourage participants to let their butterflies remind them of their prayers and of God's power to transform our lives.

Addressing Stress

Category: Learning Activity

Time: 60 to 90 minutes

Family Focus: Families will identify situations that cause stress and explore healthy ways to deal with them.

Supplies: For each family, you'll need a copy of the "Nose for the News" list (p. 27), a newspaper, and a Bible.

Give each family a newspaper and a copy of the "Nose for the News" list (p. 27). To begin, give families five minutes to look through their newspapers for each item on the "Nose for the News" list. Have family members tear out any articles and ads that match an item on the list, but tell families

Butterfly Designs

Caterpillar Stage

Pupal Stage

Butterfly Stage

Nose for the News

Find

an article in the sports section that mentions money

an article on youth culture

an article on crime in your town

an article concerning research into a deadly disease

an ad for a car that's ten years old or older

an article that mentions the president of the United States

an ad for drapery cleaning

an article that reports someone's death

an article that mentions illegal drugs

an article that describes a tragedy

an article that deals with abortion, gay rights, or prejudice

an article about your local school system

that no article or ad may be used more than once.

After five minutes, have family members each choose several of the articles their family has collected and scan each article so they will be able to briefly recount the article's contents if called upon. Then have the whole group discuss these questions:

• **Would you describe the news your group found as good news or bad news? Why?**

• **Do you agree with the saying, "No news is good news"? Why or why not?**

• **Do news articles like these increase your stress level? Why or why not?**

Say: **When stress isn't handled correctly, it can cause physical, emotional, and spiritual harm. Physically, stress causes blood vessels to constrict, resulting in headaches and other pains. Stress can also lead to ulcers and nervous disorders. Spiritually, stress can undermine your peace and joy, causing frustration, discouragement, and even despair. Today we'll look at a few causes of stress for each of us, find wisdom in the Bible to help deal with it, and then come up with practical ways to relieve the stress in our lives.**

Tell families you will read a list of potential "stressors" that happen in everyday life. After you've read each stressor, ask one person in each family to pantomime how he or she might respond to the stressor in real life. Each time you read a new stressor, have a different family member in each family pantomime a response. Anytime a person's pantomime is unclear, have him or her explain it to the whole group.

Read aloud these stressors, allowing time between each one for family members to pantomime their responses.

- It's noon when you realize you forgot to use deodorant.
- You wake up to find you have a huge pimple right on the end of your nose.
- You've just found out your job is being eliminated.
- The auto mechanic just called to tell you that it's worse than he thought—your car repair will cost at least $800.
- A close friend just died.
- The IRS just sent you a letter informing you that your tax return from two years ago is wrong and you still owe $2,000 plus penalties and interest.
- You've just been yelled at by your boss (or teacher) for making a stupid mistake.
- You've been passed over for a big promotion that you thought you deserved.

After the pantomimes, have participants discuss these questions with their families:

- Which of these situations would cause you the most stress? Why?
- How well do you handle stress? Explain.
- What is one area in your life in which you are experiencing the most stress? Explain.

Have families look up the following verses and discuss how each applies to stress management: Matthew 6:34; Luke 12:22-34; Romans 8:28; and Philippians 4:6-9. Then have families discuss these questions:

- How does your faith in God help you manage stress?
- What's one way you can apply the Scriptures we've just read to reduce your stress?
- What other words of encouragement can you offer family members who are going through stressful times?

Have family groups close by praying for one another, asking God to help each family member cast his or her anxieties on Christ and to learn to walk in God's peace.

....

Taking It Home

Each evening this week, have family members create a "shoulder massage circle" and massage one another's shoulders for ten minutes. During that time, have each family member share any "stressors" that occurred that day. Close the massage time by praying for one another.

....

Put the Cards on the Table

Category: Learning Activity

Time: 40 to 60 minutes

Family Focus: Family members will discover a new way to open conversations about conflicts.

Supplies: You'll need one deck of cards for each family group and a Bible.

As participants arrive, instruct them to sit together in a circle with their family. Give each family a deck of cards, and have each family member pull one card from the deck.

Say: **Go around your family circle and take turns sharing one pet peeve you have that's related to your family. For example, maybe you don't like the way your family keeps the house so messy, or perhaps you wish certain members of your family would stop drinking milk straight from the carton. The person with the highest card should go first. If two or more people have cards of the same value, put your cards back in the deck and draw again.**

When families have finished, read aloud Matthew 18:15, then invite families to discuss these questions:

• **What are some things that cause struggles in families?**

• **How do people deal with family conflict?**

family-friendly Advice

This is a "high-risk" family activity. You'll be asking the participants to open themselves up for potentially emotional discussions. Be careful to encourage everyone to use the simplest conflicts for the practice session that you will lead them through.

• What are some difficulties you've faced in your family?

• How does your family deal with conflicts when they come up?

• What's difficult about dealing with conflict?

Allow ten minutes for discussion, then get everyone's attention and say: Every family faces conflicts. In fact, every person faces conflicts. There are few who enjoy a conflict, but some people deal with conflict better than others do. Often the hardest part of dealing with conflict is beginning the conversation. Today we'll learn a new way to open the door to discussion about problems we have with one another in our families.

Each group has been given a deck of cards. These cards will represent struggles we have with members of the family. Small-numbered cards are for small issues—little annoying things like leaving cabinet doors open or leaving the cap off the toothpaste tube. Big-numbered cards represent more serious concerns, such as not paying attention when you're told to do something or teasing another member of the family. Finally, the face cards represent serious hurts, such as lying or breaking a trust.

In your family group, you will practice a way to open the conversation about a conflict you have.

To begin, have family members each think of a problem or concern they have with another member of the family. For the purpose of this activity, have family members limit their concerns to "small-numbered cards" only. Those are the lowest level concerns. When each person has a concern he or she would like to address, have family members each select a card and hand it to the person they want to talk to. Then have family members take turns explaining their concerns. Encourage them to specifically describe the behaviors they're concerned about. For example, a participant might say, "When you leave the cap off of the toothpaste tube,…." and avoid using words that accuse, such as "you always" or "you never." Instead tell family members to use "I" messages, like "I think" or "I feel." For example, a person might say, "When you leave the cap off of the toothpaste tube, I feel frustrated." Then have family members explain what causes those feelings. For example, a member might say, "I feel frustrated because I tell myself that you aren't interested in keeping the bathroom neat."

Have the other person respond first by saying what he or she heard. For example, "I hear you say that when I leave the top off the toothpaste tube, you feel frustrated because you think I'm not interested in keeping a neat bathroom."

The person giving the card may then agree with the response or clarify anything that was not properly heard.

When everyone understands the instructions, say: **We'll do this activity until everyone in the group has had a chance to give and receive a card. Begin now by thinking about something you'd like to share with another member of the family. In a minute, I'll invite you to begin sharing your card.** Allow about one minute, then tell the participants to begin sharing.

This activity can work for children as young as five years old. Parents may be hesitant to try this, but encourage them to help the younger children think about some simple problem they might have to share with another family member. Be careful not to listen in on conversations, but do be aware that some "simple" concerns may lead families into more intense emotional issues. You may have to encourage some to save deeper conversations for home.

When groups have finished their discussions, or are nearly finished, stop the conversation and say: **Remember, our goal isn't to resolve the conflicts here. We're just working on a way to open the conversation. I encourage you to finish your conversations and resolve your conflicts when our time together has finished.**

Read aloud Matthew 18:15. Say: **Jesus teaches us that the best way to handle conflict is to go directly to the person with whom we have a problem. Today we've shared a simple tool to open difficult conversation. You may want to use this tool regularly as a way to keep communication open in your family.**

Close with a prayer.

....

Taking It Home

Encourage families to finish their conversations when they get home, so they can resolve their minor conflicts. Challenge families to keep a deck of cards sitting out in the living room at all times. Then encourage family members to use the cards as a way of telling another family member that they'd like to talk.

....

Family Contracts

Category: Learning Activity

Time: 1 to 2 hours

Family Focus: Families will learn how to create family contracts to help them set boundaries for good family relationships.

Supplies: You'll need paper, pencils, bordered paper with an "official document" look, and black fine-tipped markers.

When everyone has arrived, invite participants to sit in "clusters" with their families. Explain that whenever two or more people live together under the same roof, misunderstandings are bound to occur. We each have our own way of doing things, our own temperaments and abilities. Although we want to allow plenty of room for individual differences, we also want our homes to run smoothly. One way to avoid problems is to agree as a family on basic "house rules" and establish "family contracts" when necessary.

House rules are basic, simple rules of conduct that apply not only to family

Sample House Rules

Here are sample house rules developed by a family of four with two young sons, aged nine and eleven. (Notice the humor that's included!)

1. If you make a mess, clean it up. (Don't hide it. We'll forgive you.)

2. A big mess? Tell someone!

3. Whatever you play with, please put it back where it belongs when you've finished.

4. Take all food and eating stuff to the kitchen when finished.

5. No hitting, bad language, or name-calling.

6. If you need something, ask. (No, you can't have the car to go to Dairy Queen!)

7. Share, take turns, and be fair.

8. Treat others the way you want them to treat you.

members but also to visiting guests. They might be as general as "treat others the way you want them to treat you" or as specific as "return all used dishes and cups to the kitchen before you leave."

A family contract, however, is a written agreement between two or more family members that outlines specific actions to be taken by each person involved, and lists consequences for violations. It's a way for family members to literally "read off the same page."

After explaining the difference between house rules and a family contract, tell families that they will work together to create some house rules of their own. Give each family a copy of the "Sample House Rules" (p. 32). After looking over these sample house rules, ask each family to take ten minutes to write its own list of rules. Have families brainstorm first on scratch paper by writing everything that comes to mind, and by getting input from each family member. Then have families choose eight to ten house rules that everyone agrees with. Ask a family member to write them neatly with a black marker on a sheet of "official," bordered paper.

When families have finished, ask several volunteers to share some of their house rules. Congratulate families on their creativity and practicality. Then say: **Now that we have established the house rules, let's explore family contracts. Is someone in your family having a hard time getting along with another member? Try working out a contract! Here's a sample family contract between two brothers (aged nine and eleven).**

Give each family a copy of the "Sample Family Contract" (p. 33). After reading

Sample Family Contract

There are four things I plan to do to make my brother's life happier:

1. I will let my brother tell me when I'm bossy.

2. I will be polite to my brother (say "please" and "thank you").

3. I will try not to lie to my brother.

4. I will try not to put my brother down.

This is the sequence of consequences I'll experience if I violate my plans:

1. a warning from my parents,

2. fifteen minutes in my room, and

3. grounded for one or two days.

it over together, have families discuss whether they feel they might need to create a contract for some of the people in their families. Establishing a family contract is generally a good idea if

- there is a chronic problem with a relationship or a behavior;
- a family member has been deeply hurt by another member's actions; or
- a family member's behavior is putting one or more people in physical danger.

Based on these guidelines, encourage families to discuss whether a family contract might be right for them.

Close the session by having family members pray together, asking God to help them use what they've learned today to help them build healthy relationships with one another. Have each family go home with its own house rules and a copy of the sample contract.

Taking It Home

Encourage each family to post its house rules in a high-traffic area and to use them often to guide kids' (and adults') behavior in the home. Also challenge families to take time this week to work on creating any family contracts they need. Make sure contracts are taken seriously—parents should guide the discussion to arrive at reasonable and age-appropriate plans and to provide meaningful consequences for those who fail to adhere to the contract. All contracts should be signed and dated, and should include a prayer asking God's help in caring for one another.

Star-Spangled Quiz

Category: Learning Activity

Time: 30 to 40 minutes

Family Focus: Families will compete to see who knows all the lines from our national anthem.

Supplies: You'll need an American flag, paper, pencils, and copies of "The Star-Spangled Banner" (p. 37).

Display the American flag, then lead the group in singing the first part of the national anthem. Afterward, ask whether anyone knows the story behind how the national anthem was written.

Share this background information with the group: **Congress officially recognized "The Star-Spangled Banner" as the national anthem of the United States in 1931. But the song was actually written by Francis Scott Key in 1814, during a time of national crisis.**

In August of 1814, British forces set fire to the Capitol and other buildings in Washington, D.C. As they returned to their ships, they captured and took prisoner a friend of Francis Scott Key. Distraught by his friend's capture, Key set out from Baltimore aboard a ship called the *Minden,* flying a flag of truce, and set sail for the British fleet.

Key found the British ships at the mouth of the Potomac River. They were preparing to attack Baltimore. The British officers agreed to release Key's friend; but they put a guard on the *Minden* to see that the Americans did not return to port until the attack was over. On September 13, the British began to bombard Fort McHenry, which guarded Baltimore. While daylight lasted, Key could see the American flag flying over the fort. At night he could only watch the shells "bursting in air." Anxiously he paced the deck, waiting for the dawn. When daybreak finally came, Key was thrilled to see, waving in the breeze, "the star-spangled banner."

family-friendly Advice

Although this activity is designed to be used near Independence Day, it would be just as impactful any other time of the year.

While the bombardment continued, Key took a letter from his pocket and on the back of it began to write the words of a song. He finished all the verses on the way to shore, but some of the lines were only in his memory. As soon as he reached his hotel room, he wrote out the complete song as it now stands. "The Star-Spangled Banner" was favorably received in Baltimore, but only gradually found its way into song books. It did not become popular as a truly national song until the Civil War.

After sharing the background information, distribute paper and pencils to each family and give these instructions: **As a family, see how many words of** the national anthem you can recall from memory.

After several minutes, have families share their results with the whole group. Congratulate any family that remembered more than the first verse. Then distribute copies of "The Star-Spangled Banner" (p. 37) to each family. Have families read through the verses; then gather everyone together to discuss these questions:

• **What's your reaction to reading the entire song?**
• **What do you like most about the message of this song?**
• **What concerns you most as you read these lyrics?**

Read this section of the song aloud to the group: "**Blest with victory and peace, may the Heaven-rescued land Praise the Power that hath made and preserved us a nation.**" Then ask:

• **Do you think this statement reflects the attitude of most people in our nation today? Why or why not?**
• **Do you think these words reflect the attitude we should have as a nation? Why or why not?**
• **What can we do as families to help our nation turn to God?**

Close by singing together all the verses of "The Star-Spangled Banner." After the song, lead the group in a prayer for our nation, asking God to have mercy on us and to draw our nation toward him.

Taking It Home

Sometime in the coming week, encourage families to get together and brainstorm a few specific ways they can help influence our nation to turn to God. For example, a family might set aside a day for fasting and prayer for the nation, or they might volunteer to help in a political campaign for a candidate they believe in.

THE STAR-SPANGLED BANNER

O say, can you see, by the dawn's early light,
What so proudly we hailed at the twilight's last gleaming?
Whose broad stripes and bright stars, through the perilous fight,
O'er the ramparts we watched, were so gallantly streaming!
And the rockets' red glare, the bombs bursting in air,
Gave proof through the night that our flag was still there:
O say, does that star-spangled banner yet wave
O'er the land of the free and the home of the brave?

On the shore, dimly seen through the mists of the deep,
Where the foe's haughty host in dread silence reposes,
What is that which the breeze, o'er the towering steep,
As it fitfully blows, now conceals, now discloses?
Now it catches the gleam of the morning's first beam,
In full glory reflected now shines on the stream:
'Tis the star-spangled banner!
O long may it wave
O'er the land of the free and the home of the brave!

And where is that band who so vauntingly swore
That the havoc of war and the battle's confusion
A home and a country should leave us no more?
Their blood has washed out their foul footsteps' pollution.
No refuge could save the hireling and slave
From the terror of flight, or the gloom of the grave:
And the star-spangled banner in triumph doth wave
O'er the land of the free and the home of the brave!

Oh! thus be it ever, when freemen shall stand
Between their loved homes and the war's desolation!
Blest with victory and peace, may the Heaven-rescued land
Praise the Power that hath made and preserved us a nation.
Then conquer we must, for our cause it is just,
And this be our motto: "In God is our trust."
And the star-spangled banner in triumph shall wave
O'er the land of the free and the home of the brave!

Worship Experiences

The Names of the Lord

Category: Worship Experience

Time: 1 to 2 hours

Family Focus: Families will learn more about God by examining different names for God and by using the names in worship.

Supplies: You'll need poster board, paper, markers, pens, and index cards.

Read through the list of names for God provided in the box on page 39. Write each name for God and its description on a separate index card. Give each family one or more of the completed index cards. If you have more than nine families, have families team up to form no more than nine groups.

Say: **God revealed himself to Abraham and to the early believers through his names and through actions that proved he was who he said he was. Remember, these early believers did not know about God. As he revealed himself through his names and actions, they understood that he was the only true God (Jehovah-Elyon), that he was the God who provides their sustenance and blessing (Jehovah-Jireh), that he is the God who heals (Jehovah-Rapha), and many other precious truths about his nature.**

Today we will worship God by using his names. Families or teams will present

Names of God

Jehovah-Elyon: The Lord Most High (Psalm 7:17)

Jehovah-Tsidkenu: The Lord Our Righteousness (Jeremiah 23:6)

Jehovah-Shammah: The Lord Who Is Present (Ezekiel 48:35)

Jehovah-M'kaddesh: The Lord Our Holiness (Exodus 31:13)

Jehovah-Shalom: The Lord Our Peace (Judges 6:23-24)

Jehovah-Rapha: The Lord Our Healer (Isaiah 53:5)

Jehovah-Jireh: The Lord Who Provides (Genesis 22:13-14)

Jehovah-Nissi: The Lord Our Banner (Exodus 17:15-16)

Jehovah-Rohi: The Lord My Shepherd (Psalm 23:1-3)

their assigned names of God, the names' meanings, and the verses that refer to the names in one of the following ways (or in some combination of ways):

• by performing a skit (acting out the Bible story in which the name is found);

• by writing a poem or script; or

• by making a poster.

Along with this group presentation, I'd like some family members to share how God has proven himself to you in the way your name of God identifies. For example, if your group has been assigned "Jehovah-Jireh," you could share a time God provided for you when you were in need.

Have families prepare their worship presentations. Circulate, and assist families in deciding how they'll present their names of God to the group. When everyone is ready, have families share their worship presentation.

After each family has presented its name of God, ask:

• What did you most enjoy about making or hearing these presentations? Explain.

• In what ways has God proven himself to you and your family?

• How can knowing God's names deepen our love for him?

• How can knowing him in these ways encourage us and strengthen us in our daily lives?

Close with a time of worship, emphasizing God's goodness, love, and faithfulness.

Taking It Home

As families leave, challenge them to begin holding private family worship times at least once a month in their homes. During these worship times, have family members focus on one name for God and use that name as a theme for singing, praying, and learning together about God's nature.

The Light of the World

Category: Worship Experience

Time: 1 to 2 hours

Family Focus: Families will enjoy making small stained-glass candles that can be used for worship in church or at home.

Supplies: A supply of small, heat-resistant glasses; tubes of liquid leading; translucent paints and brushes; wicks and wax crystals; tablespoons; containers of water; and matches. Check your craft store or hobby catalogs for discounted supplies of these items.

Invite everyone to sing together "This Little Light of Mine," "You Light Up My Life," or other songs that remind us that Jesus is the Light of the world.

If your budget permits, have each person make his or her own stained-glass candle. If funds are limited, assign one or two candles per family. There are enough steps in this activity for each person to have some creative input.

Distribute the heat-resistant glasses. Show pictures of stained-glass designs from books, magazines, or craft catalogs. Explain that some stained-glass windows tell a story—each window depicting a scene from the Bible or illustrating scenes from the life of Jesus.

Make sure each group or person has a supply of liquid leading (usually in a tube), translucent paints and brushes, a container of water, a tablespoon, wax crystals, and a wick. The leader should keep all the matches until the activity is near completion and then distribute them only to adults.

Use the liquid leading to outline a design on your glass. Broad-petaled flowers, hearts, and mosaic shapes all work well. Leave plenty of space between the lines for painting.

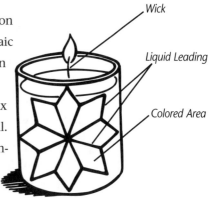

While the leading dries, carefully spoon in wax crystals to fill the glass approximately one-third full. Insert the wick, and continue to add wax crystals until the glass is filled two-thirds full. Leave the wick exposed about one-fourth inch above the wax.

Choose your colors, and paint within the lines to create a beautiful "stained-glass" effect. Allow several minutes for the paint to dry. When everyone has finished, distribute matches to the adults. Darken the room, light each candle, and sing "Behold What Manner of Love," "The Coloring Song," or other worship songs about the light of God's love, power, and majesty.

Taking It Home

Suggest that families light their candles during family worship time. Rotate the assignment of lighting the candle each night, and ask older children to use their concordances to look up verses that feature the word "light." If a family has several candles, use one as a gift to neighbors and attach a note thanking them for "lighting up your neighborhood."

Birthday Worship

Category: Worship Experience

Time: 1 to 2 hours

Family Focus: Family members will recall their birthdays and worship Jesus on his birthday.

Supplies: For each family, you'll need Bibles, a clear glass Christmas ornament (with an opening in the top), construction paper, crayons, permanent markers, scissors, and ornament hooks. You'll also need a large birthday cake and a small undecorated Christmas tree.

Before the meeting begins, separate each family's supplies and lay the supplies on tables. As families arrive, ask them to sit together around a batch of supplies. Give a glass ornament to an adult in each family. When everyone is seated, say: **Today we're going to celebrate our birthdays, even though it may not be your birthday. In just a moment, I want each person to use the construction paper I've provided to create something that reminds you of your birthday. For example, if you were born in July, you might make a red, white, and blue flag. If you were born in the fall, you might make a brightly colored leaf. These shapes can be drawn, colored, cut, or torn out of construction paper.** Invite families to start, and remind them that they have only a few minutes.

When several groups have neared completion, say: **Now I'd like each person to share the shape with your family and tell why it reminds you of your birthday.**

After everyone has shared, have families open their Bibles to Luke 2:1-15 and have someone in each family read the passage. After the reading, have participants discuss these questions with their families:

family-friendly Advice

Be sure to prepare enough birthday cake so everyone can have a piece.

• **How was the birth of Jesus like your birthday?**

• **How was Jesus' birthday different from yours?**

• **What are some ways you celebrate your birthday?**

• **What are some ways we celebrate Jesus' birthday?**

After the discussion, say: **Jesus is God. He was born into a family and became a human being like you and me. In fact, the Bible tells us that Jesus called Christians his brothers and sisters. An adult in your group has a glass Christmas ornament. I'd like you to carefully remove the top of that ornament. Each family member will place his or her birthday shape inside this ornament. If your shape is too large, cut a smaller piece from it and place it in the ornament.** Allow time for families to complete this assignment.

Say: **Replace the top on the ornament, and with the permanent marker, write the initials of each family member on the outside of the glass. This ornament is a reminder of Jesus' birthday. Inside are reminders of our birthdays. In**

Jesus, all who believe are members of the same family. What a wonderful reason to celebrate.

Invite everyone to have a piece of cake. After the cake has been served, lead families in singing "Happy Birthday" to Jesus, followed by several other worship songs focusing on Christ's birth. For your closing, have families take turns hanging their ornaments on the Christmas tree and offering a prayer of worship and thanks to God for sending his Son to live among us. When all the families have offered a prayer and hung their ornaments, invite everyone to form a circle around the tree and sing a closing worship song.

Allow families to take their ornaments home as reminders to celebrate Jesus' birthday and to worship him this Christmas season.

Taking It Home

Invite families to hang their ornaments on their Christmas trees every year as reminders of God's gift of families and his gift of Jesus, born as a baby so long ago.

The Secret of Peace

Category: Worship Experience

Time: 1 to 2 hours

Family Focus: Families will discover how to have peace with God and one another.

Supplies: You'll need Bibles, worship songs, paper, and colored markers or pens.

This is an intergenerational worship experience. After everyone has arrived, begin by singing a few worship songs. Then invite a high school student to lead the whole group in prayer.

Next, ask for two volunteers who are under the age of twelve. Ask each volunteer to read one of these verses to the whole group: Song of Songs 2:4 and Psalm 5:11.

Thank the children, then say: **Today we'll be talking about eternal treasures— treasures that will last forever. Today, the eternal treasure we'll explore is peace. We're going to discover the secret of peace.**

Ask for two volunteers who are over the age of sixty to each read aloud one of these verses: Isaiah 26:3 and John 14:27. After the reading, ask the whole group:

- **How many of you have experienced pain?**
- **How do you usually deal with pain?**
- **Is it possible to have peace when you are in pain? Why or why not?**

Say: **Jesus gives an inner peace that lets Christians face danger and suffering without fear or trembling hearts. Through Jesus, inner peace is possible, no matter how wild or crazy the external situation is.**

Ask:

- **How have you experienced the peace of God in your life?**

Say: **The secret of peace is knowing that, even though you can't see him now, God is with you and he is in control. He will take care of you. I'd like you to get together with your family for a few minutes and discuss these questions:**

- **What helps you have peace in life?**
- **What disrupts peace for you?**
- **How can your family help you have peace?**

After the discussion, distribute paper and colored markers or pens, and have families work together to draw a picture of "peace in the family." Make sure each family member participates in the experience. When families have finished, have them take turns sharing their creations with at least two other families. Then say: **The secret of peace is found in remembering that God is with you and that he is always in control. Nothing rattles him, so nothing needs to rattle you either. You and your family are in his hands.**

Lead families in two or three more worship songs that focus on God's peace and his help in tough times. Between each song, encourage volunteers to pray for God's peace in their families.

After the worship time, close with prayer and invite families to hang their drawings on their refrigerators as reminders of God's peace.

Challenge participants, within their families, to memorize John 14:27 and to work together to create a list of practical ways they can remind one another that Jesus is always with them and is always in control. Encourage each family member to choose one idea from the list and do it this week.

Rising Above Life's Circumstances

Category: Worship Experience

Time: 40 to 60 minutes

Family Focus: Families will experience a Thanksgiving activity that helps them focus on God's attributes and deeds.

Supplies: For each family, you'll need Bibles, and a toy balsa-wood airplane kit. You'll also need a yo-yo.

When everyone has arrived, stand up and play with the yo-yo. As you play, say: **Sometimes life doesn't go the way we hope it will. How can we rise above the circumstances of life? How can we avoid the trap of being like a yo-yo—up and down, inconsistent, always reacting to what happens—to be more like an airplane, built to rise above good and bad?**

Stop playing with the yo-yo, then say: **Job knew how to rise above the circumstances of life. In the middle of horrible pain, he praised God. Let's see how he did it.**

Have families read Job 1:20-22 together. After the reading, have families discuss these questions:

- **How did Job rise above the pain of circumstance?**
- **How can we follow Job's example in our own lives?**

Family-Friendly Advice

Although this activity is designed for the Thanksgiving season, it can be used just as effectively any time of year.

Family-Friendly Advice

If some of your participants aren't familiar with the pain Job endured, take a few moments to explain the background of Job's story by having a volunteer read aloud Job 1:1-19.

Give each family a toy airplane kit, and have families put together the toy airplanes. When they've completed their planes, have family members take turns gliding the plane to one another. Each time someone throws it, have that person say one thing he or she praises God for—based on one of the these categories:

• **recalling God's attributes** (He is good, loving, kind, powerful, faithful, and so on.)

• **remembering his works** (He sent Jesus to save us, forgives our sins, and so on.)

• **giving thanks to God** (He loves me, accepts me, takes care of me, guides me, and so on.)

Conclude the time by having families pray together, thanking God for his goodness.

After the prayer, say: **Rising above our circumstances is a lot like flying these planes. Instead of getting bogged down with the weight of our worries, we can turn our hearts upward and let God help us soar above our circumstances. Worship beats worry every time.**

Taking It Home

Throughout the coming week, encourage families to bring the airplanes to mealtimes. As family members pray for the meal, have them toss the plane around and continue to thank and to praise God for things.

Musical Montage

Category: Worship Experience

Time: 1 to 2 hours

Family Focus: Family members will choose a song to lip-sync or to perform for the rest of the group.

Supplies: You'll need several CD or cassette players and several CDs or cassettes containing a wide variety of Christian worship music. You'll also need Bibles, and to think of a few worship songs that are familiar to your families.

S et up the room with several CD players. Have each family sit together in a circle on the floor around one of the players. If you have more families than CD players, just have families team up for this activity. Make sure you have more than enough CDs available. If people bring their own CDs, make sure they've marked the CDs with their names.

When everyone is seated, say: **Welcome to our musical montage. Today we're going to worship the Lord in a different way. The first thing I want you to do in your groups is to talk about the types of music you like.**

Ask:

• **How many different types of music do your family members like?**

• **What's your favorite kind of music? Why?**

• **What's your least favorite kind of music? Why?**

Say: **Now that we know what different types of music each of us likes, as a family choose a Christian group and song that you all like. Perhaps you already have a favorite group or song. As a family, listen to a few different songs and then choose the one you all agree upon.**

Give family members several minutes to listen to songs

family-friendly Advice

Don't limit your musical selection to only music you like. Consider the variety of people in your group. Also, the week before this activity, you may encourage people to bring their CD or cassette players and their favorite worship CDs or cassettes to this event.

and to choose one they all like. After each family has chosen a favorite, bring everyone together and ask:

• **What does your family like most about your chosen song?**

• **What's message does the song convey?**

• **Why is a song's message important?**

Say: **Let's open our Bibles to Psalm 100. This passage may be familiar to some of you. It's a psalm of worship, giving thanks to God. I'd like for someone to read this passage to everyone.** Have someone read the psalm. After the reading, ask:

• What do you think is the "big message" of this psalm? Explain.

• Why do you think the psalmist proclaimed that message?

• Based on this psalm, how should we worship God?

Say: **Now that we've seen what the psalmist said regarding worship, let's take some time to worship God together.**

Lead the group in singing a few worship songs that are familiar to everyone. After the singing, say: **Now we're going to have some fun with our praise. Praising God can be really fun and joyful. The reason I had each family choose a song is because you're going to present your song to the rest of the families. I'll give you several minutes to practice your songs. When you present them, you can either lip-sync or sing along with the artists. Remember, this is a time of praise, so enjoy praising the Lord and have a good time, too.**

Give the groups several minutes to practice their songs, then let the family that's wearing the most red go first. Continue until every family has had an opportunity to present its song. Make sure you encourage everyone to clap for each family.

Say: **Thank you for your presentations. As we can see, we can praise the Lord in many different ways. Good music can help us express ourselves to God and to others.**

In closing, have families form one large circle, then go around the circle and have each person say the name of his or her favorite song or music group. After you've gone all the way around the circle, say: **Wow! That's quite a variety of musical tastes! But even in such a diverse world of opinions, we can find unity through worship. Let's close our time by worshipping once more together.**

Lead families in singing together a simple worship song, such as "Lord You Are," "Isn't He," or something similar.

Taking It Home

Encourage family members to set aside time this week to listen to one another's music. Suggest that they use dinnertime to play a few songs during each meal. The person who plays the music may then explain why he or she likes that type of music and what the lyrics say to him or her.

Piling On

Category: Worship Experience

Time: 40 to 60 minutes

Family Focus: Families will share in a confessional worship experience.

Supplies: You'll need stacks of magazines and newspapers (thirty or more per family), a Bible, masking tape, and a large cross. For each person, you'll need a white carnation.

Before participants arrive, set several tables along one wall with stacks of magazines and newspapers piled on them. Across from and parallel to the tables, place a line of masking tape on the floor as a starting line. Place the cross in an isolated part of the room, and use the carnations to decorate the area around the cross.

After families have arrived, say: **To lead into our time of worship, we will begin with a relay race. Each family will line up behind the tape line. On "go," the youngest person in your family will cross the room to the tables and pick up as many magazines as possible, then return across the room, and hand the pile to the next oldest person. While still holding the magazines, that person will cross the room and add to the pile without setting it down, return, and hand the pile to the next oldest person. The game ends when the last person brings the pile back across the tape line or when someone in your group drops the pile of magazines.**

When families understand the rules, begin the relay. Encourage participants to pile on as many magazines as they can—you want the piles to be as unwieldy as possible.

When families have finished the relay, ask each family to sit together in a circle and discuss the following questions:

• **What happened in this activity?**
• **What did you find challenging?**

Ask for reports from the groups. Read aloud 1 John 1:8-9, then ask families to discuss these questions:

- **How was this game like carrying the guilt of sin?**
- **How do we get rid of that burden?**

As families discuss these questions, walk around the room and give each participant a magazine. Regain their attention, and say: **As we reflect on what happens in our lives when we carry a load of sin and guilt, let's prepare our hearts to hear God's Word.** To prepare people's hearts for the closing activity, lead the group in songs that have a confession or forgiveness theme.

After the singing, say: **The magazine you're holding represents the guilt of sin you carry when you don't confess your sins to God. Take a moment of silence and reflect on those sins you haven't confessed. In a moment, I'll invite the oldest member of your group to say a prayer, asking God to forgive our sins and free us from the burden of guilt.** Allow time, then initiate the prayer.

When prayer ceases, say: **Hear this from God's Word.** Read aloud 1 John 1:1-2. Say: **You're invited, at this time, to come to the cross. Leave your magazine on the floor as a symbol that Jesus has taken away your sins, and take a white carnation as a reminder that you have received God's forgiveness. You may come forward when you're ready.** As people come forward, quietly play worshipful music or repeat singing one of the earlier songs. Allow time for everyone who wishes to leave his or her magazine and come forward. Close with a prayer and a final worship song.

Taking It Home

Encourage families to take home their white carnations. Have them place their carnations on their dining room tables as reminders that Jesus' death on the cross has paid the price for their sins.

Rock On

Category: Worship Experience

Time: 1 to 2 hours

Family Focus: Families will learn about altars and will use them as they worship together.

Supplies: For each person, you'll need a medium-sized, flat rock. You'll also need Bibles, markers, several large rocks, pens, and paper.

Before the event, stack the larger stones in the center of the room. As people enter, say: **Please sit in a group around the stack of rocks.** After everyone has been seated, say: **Today we'll learn about some altars in the Bible and why they were built. Then we'll create our own altar and worship together.**

Distribute pens and paper, then have participants take out their Bibles. Assign each family one of the following Scriptures: Genesis 8; Genesis 12; Exodus 17; Judges 6; 1 Samuel 14; 2 Samuel 24; and 1 Kings 18. It's okay if more than one family has the same Scripture or if not all the Scriptures are assigned. Say: **I want you to read your assigned passage and answer the following questions:**

- **Who built the altar?**
- **Why did they build it?**
- **What did God do for them?**
- **Where was the altar located?**

Give families several minutes to work, and make sure they write their answers on their paper.

When families have finished, say: **Let's share with one another what we found out about our altars.** Give each family an opportunity to share with the rest of the group. After everyone has shared, say: **That really helped us to see what God did for each of these people and what the people did to help them remember his faithfulness. Now, turn back to your families and discuss these questions:**

• What do we do today to remember God's faithfulness in our lives?

• Do others know about the things God has done in your lives? Why or why not?

After the discussion, say: **In each of our passages, God did something either through or for the people who built the altar. Their altar was there to remind them and others of God's faithfulness. Today, we'll work together to create a worship altar of our own.**

Have families discuss this question:

• **What's one important way God has shown his love, power, or faithfulness in your life?**

As families discuss, give each person a medium-sized, flat stone and a marker. When they've finished their discussion, have each family form a circle. Then say: **Now that we've all shared, on the flat part of your rock, write the verse you've chosen. After you've written the verse, combine your family's stones to create a "family altar" on the floor in the center of your circle.**

When families have done this, have them kneel around their family altar and place their hands on the rocks. Encourage families to spend time worshipping God together, thanking him for the ways he has demonstrated his faithfulness, power, and love in their lives.

After allowing several minutes for families to worship, say: **Creating altars with your family is a great way to worship. But as Christians, we are each part of a larger family. To close our worship time, let's combine our altars together to create a lasting memorial to God's faithfulness in our lives.**

Have family members collect their rocks, then guide participants outside to a place where they can build a more permanent altar. Using their rocks, have families work together to construct one altar.

When families have completed the altar, have them gather around the altar and join hands. Say: **Repeat the following prayer aloud as I pray: Dear God, thank you for your faithfulness.** (Repeat.) **Thank you for the altars in our lives that help us remember your love and your power.** (Repeat.) **Help me to show love to others the way** you have shown your love to me. (Repeat.) **Thank you for this altar and for what it represents to each of us.** (Repeat.) **We praise you, Lord.** (Repeat.) **In Jesus' name, amen.** (Repeat.)

After the prayer, dismiss the group.

Taking It Home

Suggest that families continue building altars together at home. Encourage them to take several smaller rocks and keep them available at home. Each time God does something to demonstrate his faithfulness to their family, encourage them to build a small altar as an act of worship and a reminder of what God has done.

Family Communion

Category: Worship Experience

Time: 30 to 40 minutes

Family Focus: Families will celebrate the Lord's Supper together.

Supplies: For each family, you'll need a Bible and a large paper sack. In each sack, place the elements of the Lord's Supper, cups, and napkins. Before the activity, give each family a damp washcloth.

Have each family find its own area in the meeting room and sit in a circle. Say: **Before he died, Jesus shared one last meal with his disciples. At that meal, he asked that his followers regularly participate in a communion meal together, in remembrance of him. Today, we're going to celebrate the Lord's Supper in our families so we can better understand the significance of his death and resurrection.**

Read aloud Mark 14:12-16. Then say: **Send one of your family members here to get the things you'll need for communion.** Have each person take back to his or her family one of the paper sacks you've prepared. Have families set out the napkins, cups, and elements of the Lord's Supper.

When families have prepared their communion meals, read aloud Mark 14:17-21. Then say: **We are born sinful and live in a sinful world. Each of us has turned away from Christ. In humility and gratitude for his sacrifice on the cross, let's ask Jesus to wash away our sins.**

Have family members take turns wiping their hands with the damp washcloth while asking Jesus to forgive them for the sins they have committed. Encourage family members to be specific in their confessions. After each person prays, have him or her pass the washcloth to the next family member in the circle. Continue until everyone has asked for Christ's forgiveness.

Read aloud Mark 14:22. Instruct family members to break and eat their bread (or wait for the minister to serve them). Then say: **As you eat your bread, take turns completing this prayer aloud, "Jesus, thank you for..."** Encourage family members to thank Jesus for specific things he has done in their lives, such as "helping me share Christ at school," or "helping me to stop smoking."

After eating the bread, read aloud Mark 14:23-25. Instruct families to drink together (or wait for the minister to serve them). Then say: **As you drink, take turns completing this prayer aloud, "Jesus, help me to..."** Encourage family members to ask Christ's help for specific struggles in their lives. For example, "Help me to be more bold in sharing my faith at work," or "Help me to serve my family more humbly."

When families have finished, read aloud Mark 14:26. Say: **Just as the original disciples ended their meal with a song, let's end our meal by praising God together.**

Close by leading families in singing a worship song or hymn such as "At the Cross," or "I Am the Resurrection."

Taking It Home

As part of their family devotional time, encourage families to celebrate the Lord's Supper together as a family on a regular basis. During family communion, encourage family members to open up with one another about specific reasons they are thankful to God, and specific struggles for which they need God's help.

Jesus Is in the House

Category: Worship Experience

Time: 40 to 60 minutes

Family Focus: Family members will work together to welcome Jesus into their home and hearts.

Supplies: You'll need Bibles, paper, pencils, glue, scissors, colored paper, markers, tape, poster board, a CD player, and assorted worship-music CDs.

When everyone has arrived, say: **Today we have a special guest coming to join us, and I want us to take some time to prepare for his arrival. First, let me give you a clue about who he is.**

Read aloud Mark 11:1-11 with enthusiasm. Then say: **Today we're going to welcome Jesus into our meeting place, perhaps similar to the way the people of Jerusalem welcomed him to their city. As part of our welcoming celebration, each family will prepare a portion of the experience.**

Give each family a sheet of paper and a pencil. Have a family member divide the paper into two columns and title one, "What we can offer" and the other, "What we can do." Instruct family members to brainstorm what they (as a family) can offer to Jesus that would be pleasing to him, and what they can do (in this experience) to welcome him into your meeting.

While families brainstorm, set out all the supplies you've gathered before the activity. After several minutes, instruct family members to use their list as a springboard to create a two-minute presentation to welcome Jesus into their family. For example, families might say a group prayer of devotion, sing a song of worship and surrender, or openly commit themselves to serving Christ in their families. Tell families they can use any of the supplies you have gathered, including any of the worship songs you've collected.

When families are ready, place an empty chair in the center of the room and tell families to imagine that Jesus has just arrived and is sitting in the chair. One at a time, have families offer their welcoming presentations to Jesus. After all the presentations, have all the families join together in singing a few worship songs or hymns, welcoming Jesus into their midst.

After the songs, gather everyone together and ask:

• **How did you feel as you gave your presentation to Jesus?**

• **How is this experience similar to the way we should welcome Jesus into our hearts every day?**

• **How might this experience be similar to the way we should welcome Jesus into our homes every day?**

• **What are some things you can do as a family to make Jesus feel more welcome in your home?**

Close by having families pray for one another, asking God to show them how they can make Jesus feel welcome in their homes every day.

Taking It Home

Challenge families to take this idea home by going through their homes together and removing anything that might make Jesus uncomfortable. For example, families might decide to throw out movies that Jesus wouldn't want them to watch, or they might commit to limiting their television viewing to only certain programs that honor God. Challenge families to take their commitments one step further by "redecorating" their foyers or entryways to represent their desire to welcome Jesus into their homes. Family members might do this by hanging significant Bible passages on the walls, or by displaying a Bible to represent their desire to honor Jesus in all they do within their household.

Stations of Prayer

Category: Worship Experience

Time: 20 to 30 minutes

Family Focus: Family members will learn about different kinds of prayer.

Supplies: You'll need four tables. For each table, you'll need a Bible, and several candles. You'll also need paper, pens, matches, a CD player, and some quiet worship music to play in the background.

Before the activity, set up four stations at different places in your church or meeting room. Place several lit candles at each station, along with one or two Bibles. Also, at each station, place a sheet of paper with one of the following words and instructions written on it:

Station 1—Praise. Tell God why you think he's wonderful! Say a prayer, read a psalm, or sing a song of praise.

Station 2—Thanks. Thank God for what he's done for you and for your family. Read a favorite Bible verse that reminds you to be thankful.

Station 3—Request. Tell God your needs and the needs of others.

Station 4—Confession. Read 1 John 1:9. Tell God you're sorry for the things you've done wrong, and ask him to forgive you.

After families have arrived, dim the lights and play some quiet worship music in the background. Give each family member a sheet of paper and a pen. Have participants divide their papers into four sections and label each section with one of these titles: "Praise," "Thanks," "Request," and "Confession."

Have participants fill in each section according to these instructions:

• In the Praise section, write what you think it means to praise God, and then list at least three things you'd like to praise God for in your life.

• In the Thanks section, write at least five things you're thankful to God for.

• In the Request section, write at least two things you'd like God to do for you, and two things you'd like him to do for someone you love.

• In the Confession section, write any attitudes or actions you need to ask God's forgiveness for in your life.

When families have finished their papers, send them to different prayer stations (it's OK if there are more than one family at each station). Instruct family members to share with God and one another what they've written on their papers, and to follow the instructions provided at that station. Explain that families should remain at each station and pray as directed for about five minutes. (You can make this time shorter if you have younger children, or longer if you have older children.) After five minutes, have families move to a different station.

Challenge family members to remain in an attitude of prayer and worship as they visit each station. Encourage them to huddle close together as they pray and share, so as not to disturb other families that may be at the same station or a nearby station.

Continue the worship time until all the families have visited each of the stations. Then gather everyone together, and have participants discuss these questions with their families:

• **How did it feel to go through this worship experience as a family?**

• **Was it hard to share your requests or confess your sins in front of your family? Why or why not?**

• **What did this experience teach you about prayer or worship?**

• **How could praying regularly with your family in this way strengthen your relationships with one another?**

• **How could regular family prayer and worship strengthen your relationship with God?**

After the discussion time, gather all the families together and ask them to share with the whole group what they've discovered through this experience. Then have families all join hands, and close by singing one or two songs of praise or thanks to God.

Taking it Home

Challenge families to begin praying and worshipping together on a regular basis at home. Suggest they begin with a four-week commitment to gather together as a family once a week for prayer and worship. At the end of the four weeks, have family members discuss how the prayer time has helped them and how they can continue to strengthen their relationship with God and with one another through regular family prayer times.

Adapted from an activity titled "Stations of Prayer" in
52 Fun Family Prayer Adventures (Augsburg) by Mike and Amy Nappa.

Service Projects

Cool Yule Caroling and Progressive Feast

Category: Service Project

Time: 3 to 4 hours

Family Focus: This activity will bring Christmas cheer to elderly, shut-in members of the congregation as well as to participating families.

Supplies: You'll need copies of popular Christmas carols (with both lyrics and notes); flashlights (at least one for every two people); a complete meal in three courses (appetizer, main course, and dessert); and three host homes big enough to house all participants.

Before the event, find three host homes and assign each host a different course of the "feast" to serve—appetizer, main course, or dessert. Ask each host family to organize all the preparation for its assigned portion of the meal.

On a map, mark the locations of all the host homes. Then using a different-colored pen, mark the locations of

Family-Friendly Advice

Your church could cover the cost of the food by charging participants a few dollars for the event.

the elderly church members or other people you'd like participants to visit. Using this information, create a route that takes participants to each of the host homes in turn, with several caroling stops in between.

On the night of the event, distribute copies of the Christmas carols and be sure carolers have flashlights (at least one for every two people). Practice the songs with the group. Afterward, lead the group in prayer, asking God to let the songs you sing bring Christmas joy and cheer to those who hear them.

When everyone is ready, distribute maps of the route, then send families on their way.

Taking It Home

After the final course, challenge families to go caroling again sometime before Christmas—only this time have them carol in their own neighborhoods. Encourage them to share a bag of Christmas cookies with each of the families they visit.

Gather, Sack, 'n' Pray

Category: Service Project

Time: 2 to 3 hours

family Focus: Families will reach out to the poor with food and prayer.

Supplies: You'll need assorted groceries, collected from church members, and brown paper sacks.

Before this project, select a low-income neighborhood in your area that you'd like to reach with God's love. A week before the service project, go to the neighborhood and distribute fliers, letting residents know you will be offering free groceries the following week and asking whether they want to receive any. The flier should explain what you are doing and why, and make it clear that there are no strings attached—the food is free. You should also include the church address, the church phone number, and the time you will be there to distribute the food. Tell those interested in receiving groceries to call the church office and leave their names and addresses, along with messages indicating that they would like groceries delivered to their homes the following week.

Let church members know the kind of foods you are looking for—nonperishable food items work best. Accept monetary donations as well, so you can buy any items that church members didn't supply. A few days before the event, gather all the food together. Then use the monetary donations to purchase anything else you need.

The day of the project, have families begin by placing all the groceries in bags—with the same assortment of foods in each bag. Then have families head out to the neighborhood you plan to serve. Give each family a list of addresses to visit, along with the appropriate number of grocery bags. As families give away the groceries, encourage them to ask the residents whether they have any needs for which the team can pray. If possible, have families pray with the residents right then. Otherwise, have families keep track of residents' prayer requests, so they can be prayed for later. After all the groceries have been distributed, have families return to the church.

When everyone has arrived back at the church, lead the group in a time of praise and worship, thanking God for his goodness. Then have families report any highlights or lessons they've learned from this experience. Close by praying together for the requests of the families you've visited.

Taking It Home

As they leave, challenge families to consider "tithing" their groceries—giving away one tenth of what they buy to the poor or to those who are hungry. As a further expression of identification with the poor and hungry around them, challenge families to fast for a meal or two each week as well—and spend that time praying for the needs of people they know.

Blessings Box

Category: Service Projects

Time: 1 to 2 hours

Family Focus: Many community agencies like the American Cancer and Heart Associations use volunteers such as in-home hospice caregivers or drivers who transport clients to and from doctor's appointments or chemotherapy treatments. In this activity, families will make "Blessings Boxes" to thank these tireless workers.

Supplies: You'll need cardboard shoe boxes; decorative wrapping paper; tissue paper; scotch tape; scissors; coffee mugs (or a similar gift item); individual tissue packs; Life-Savers™; small containers of bottled water; notepads; pencils; thank you cards; and gift certificates to a local car wash, restaurant, or bookstore.

Prior to this activity, call your local American Cancer or Heart Association. Tell the representative you are interested in having someone from the agency visit your church for "Family Night." Explain that you would like the agency to provide a short talk on the overall work of the agency, especially highlighting the work of volunteers.

Ask the agency of your choice for the number and first names of their volunteers, and tell them you will be providing special "Blessings Boxes" for each volunteer.

At the family night, have the visitor from the agency talk about volunteers in his or her organization. Then ask several children to read Luke 10:30-36. Ask:

• **Which of the three men was a good neighbor?**

• **How is volunteering for a community agency being a good neighbor?**

• **What can we do to serve the people who serve others so faithfully?**

Give the name of a volunteer to each family. Distribute to each group a cardboard box; enough wrapping paper to cover the box; tape; tissue paper; scissors;

Family-Friendly Advice

Although this service project is aimed at community service volunteers, the same concept would also work well for serving area pastors, youth workers, or other Christian volunteers.

one coffee mug (or other gift); a container of bottled water; a notepad; pencil; tissue pack; a pack of LifeSavers; and a gift certificate to a local car wash, restaurant, or bookstore; along with any other items you'd like to include.

Tell families to cover the box with wrapping paper and then arrange the gift items and tissue paper inside. Be sure the gift certificate has been signed. Ask a family member to write a personal note on the thank you card and to attach it to the outside of the box. Have each family address the card to its assigned volunteer.

When families have completed the boxes, either give the boxes to the agency representative who visits your church or ask whether some of your members may deliver them to the volunteers during the week.

Taking It Home

Challenge family members to add the name of their assigned agency volunteer to their personal prayer lists. Remember the volunteers by asking God to bless them for their unselfish service and to keep them safe as they serve others.

Gingerbread Joy

Category: Service Project

Time: 2 to 3 hours

Family Focus: Families will bake supersized gingerbread cookies to give away to members who are missing or shut-in.

Supplies: You'll need a standard recipe for gingerbread cookies, enough ingredients to make one supersized cookie for each recipient, icing, and cookie decorations such as sprinkles or raisins. You'll also need decorated paper plates, colored plastic wrap, stationery to write personal notes, masking tape, pens, plastic gloves, and the addresses of church members who are shut-in or missing.

Several days before the event, tell participating families that they need to bring the following baking supplies to the meeting: two large mixing bowls, a few mixing spoons, a measuring cup, measuring spoons, and two or three large cookie sheets. In addition to any ovens you may have at the church, make arrangements to use the ovens of church members who live close to your church campus. (If you don't have access to local ovens, have families take their cookies home to bake them before delivering them to their assigned members who are missing or shut-in.)

Before families arrive for the event, use masking tape to create an outline of a giant human shape on the floor. Make it large enough so participants can stand inside it. Then form a circle of chairs around the body. As families arrive, have them sit in the chairs.

family-friendly Advice

When collecting ingredients, keep in mind that one supersized gingerbread cookie is roughly equivalent to one dozen regular-sized cookies.

When everyone has arrived, read aloud 1 Corinthians 12:27. Then say: **Every one of us is an important part of our church family. If one of us were missing, part of the church body would be missing. If you were to pick one part of the body that describes how you fit in the church, what part would it be?**

Some people like to sing or share Jesus through talking. They are like a tongue in the body of Christ. Some people like helping others, reaching out in acts of service. They are like hands. Still others find their greatest contribution to the church body is to pray fervently for those in need. They are like knees. What part of the body best describes you?

Have family members stand on the part of the body shape that corresponds to their roles in the body of Christ. When everyone has chosen a place, have several volunteers complete this statement: "In the body of Christ, I am like a [fill in the blank], because I like to [fill in the blank]."

After several volunteers have shared, say: **There are parts of our body that are missing—some by choice, others not by choice. The Bible says in 1 Corinthians 12:26, "If one part suffers, every part suffers with it; if one part is honored, every part rejoices with it." The Bible also tells us, "Therefore, as we have opportunity, let us do good to all people, especially to those who belong to the family of believers" (Galatians 6:10).**

We need to let every part of the body of Christ in our church family know he or she is special. One way we can do this is to bring him or her a gift. I have collected the ingredients to bake giant gingerbread cookies to share with people in our church family who are shut-in or who we haven't seen in a while. I've also provided stationery for writing a note to these people. I'd like you to work as a family to mix the ingredients, make your cookies, decorate them, then deliver them to a few of our members who are shut-in or missing.

Give each family the names of two or three people to contact and visit. Then invite each family to collect enough ingredients to make one supersized gingerbread cookie for each of its assigned people.

When families have collected their ingredients, give these instructions: **As a family, I want you to mix your ingredients and create one supersized gingerbread "person" for each member you'll visit who is shut-in or missing. Then bake your cookies in one of the ovens I've provided.** (If no ovens are available locally, send families home to bake their cookies before delivering them.) **When your cookies are done, use the icing to decorate your cookies and to write a brief affirmation on each one. For example, you might write, "You are loved' or "You are special to us." Then write a special note to let the person or family for whom you are making the cookie know how much they are missed** and thought of. **Use Bible verses in your note, such as 1 Corinthians 12:27; Ephesians 4:15-16; Philippians 1:3-4; Colossians 1:3; or 1 Thessalonians 3:9.**

family-friendly Advice

For sanitary reasons, encourage family members to wear the plastic gloves as they prepare their cookies.

Before families leave to bake their cookies, close your time together by gathering around all the unbaked cookies and praying over them. Invite God to bless the people who are a part of the extended family of Christians.

Taking It Home

Have families deliver cookies to the people on their assigned list. Before going to the door, encourage families to pray for God to go ahead of them. Challenge families to reach out to the members who are shut-in or missing and to start a relationship that goes beyond this event.

Good and Plenty Trash Day

Category: Service Project

Time: 3 to 4 hours

Family Focus: Families will haul trash from a neighborhood and invite folks to visit their church.

Supplies: You'll need Bibles, Good & Plenty candy packets for each person; large envelopes or bags; assorted church promotional materials (bulletins, informational packets, and a map to the church); pencils or packs of crayons; balloons; coloring books; and personal welcome notes.

For hauling the trash, you'll need several trucks and a pair of work gloves for each family member.

Set out all the supplies before families arrive. As each family arrives, have family members work together to prepare welcome packets to give to neighbors around the church or in their neighborhoods. Have families fill the packets with snacks (such as Good & Plenty candy), informational materials about the church, crayons, coloring books for children, and whatever other items you choose.

When all the packets are ready, gather families and read Matthew 9:37-38. Then say: **God's harvest—that is, people who need Jesus—is good and plentiful. But the workers are few. He said to send out workers for his harvest. Are you ready and available to go into the harvest as one of God's workers?** Let's do it!

Have families form teams of six or fewer, and assign each team to a different section of the neighborhood you intend to visit. Tell truck drivers to patrol the visitation area and watch for families that may need their assistance. Distribute work gloves, then have families go door to door, asking whether the residents have any large trash items that

Family-Friendly Advice

Be sure to follow the regulations in your local area for hauling and disposing of large trash items.

need to be hauled away. Encourage families to ask for items that aren't normally collected by the regular trash pickup in their area, such as furniture or broken appliances. Tell residents this free service is being provided by the families in your church as a way to invite them to visit. Then give the residents a welcome packet.

After each truck has been loaded with trash, have the drivers take the trash to the local dump for disposal, then return to the visitation area. Encourage families to continue visiting homes until they've given away all of their welcome packets.

Taking It Home

As families go out to distribute the packets, remind them that when we do "good" things in the Lord's strength, God will produce "plenty" out of our loving actions. The key is acting out of our love for Jesus and for people. Encourage families to use this experience as a model for future family projects that involve doing "good" things for others.

Love Collages

Category: Service Project

Time: 2 to 3 hours

Family Focus: Together families will create a "love collage," then deliver it to a patient in the hospital.

Supplies: For each family, you'll need a large picture frame, cardboard, construction paper, glitter, assorted magazines, Valentine's Day decorations, colored markers, glue, tape, scissors, and other assorted craft supplies. You'll also need an instant-print camera with enough film to take one picture of each family.

A week or so before the event, call the nearest hospital and explain that you want to bring handmade "love" gifts to some of the patients. Ask the hospital representative to recommend specific patients who would especially appreciate a visit of this sort. Also ask about any hospital regulations concerning crowds or visiting hours, and adjust your event schedule accordingly.

As families arrive, take their pictures with an instant-print camera, then give them all the supplies they'll need for their projects. Say: **Using these supplies, I want you to work together as a family to create a "love collage" for someone who's sick and in the hospital. A love collage is simply a collection of pictures, shapes, words, or drawings that work together to tell someone in need that we love him or her and are praying for his or her recovery.**

Use your collective creativity to design and create your collage. Then place it in the frame I've provided. When we've all finished, we'll go to the local hospital and deliver our creations to people in need.

While families work, go around the room and make sure each family member participates. Also be sure each family includes its "family photo" somewhere in the collage. When families have finished, have them take turns explaining their collages to the rest of the group. Then say: **I feel a lot of love in this room right now. It's time we gave it away to some people who need it most. Let's go!**

Have families carpool to the nearest hospital, then have each family deliver its collage to a specific patient in the hospital. During the visit, encourage family members to ask the patient whether they can pray for him or her. When families have completed their visits, have them gather in the hospital lobby or back at the church. Have families share stories of their encounters, along with prayer requests for the patients they've met. Close the event by praying together for God to heal the people you've visited.

Taking It Home

As families leave, challenge them to go back to visit their specific patients again, and to pray for them regularly as long as needed.

Neighbors' Night Out

Category: Service Project

Time: 3 to 4 hours

Family Focus: Families will plan and lead an evening event for neighborhood children that will allow the children's parents a night off.

Supplies: You'll need paper, pens, a collection of children's activity or game books, and copies of the "What Did You Think?" card (p. 70).

Several weeks before this event, invite families to sign up to participate in "Neighbors Night Out," a program designed to allow neighborhood parents to take a break from parenting and to have some time for themselves. After enough families have signed up, meet together to set a date for the event (a Friday or Saturday night works best). When the date has been set, assign each family one of these responsibilities:

• Event Promotion—These families will create fliers advertising the event, will deliver the fliers door to door in the neighborhoods you want to reach, and will respond to any questions neighbors might have about the event.

• Registration and Follow-Up—These families will be responsible for registering all the children who attend the event, making sure they all get home safely, and following up with families who've participated.

• Event Planning—These families will be responsible for planning an evening of games, movies, storytelling, and other activities appropriate for a group of preschool and elementary children. You may want to provide several activity or game books to spark ideas.

• Food Planning—These families will be responsible for planning and preparing several healthy snacks for the children to enjoy.

It's OK if more than one family is assigned to each area

Family-Friendly Advice

If possible, have neighborhood participants preregister for the event, so that the planners will have a better idea of how much food to prepare and how many supplies to collect.

of responsibility, or if one family has responsibilities in more than one area. When all the responsibilities have been assigned, have families form groups according to their assigned tasks. Have families work together to plan their portion of the event. As families make their plans, have them keep these tips in mind:

• Fliers advertising the event should include the name of the church, the name of the event, a short explanation of the event, the date and time of the event, and a phone number to call for questions.

• Registration cards should include the children's name, addresses, phone numbers, parents' names, and any special information leaders should know about the children. If your church requires it, you may also want children's parents to sign standard release forms when they drop off their children at the church.

Assist families in any way you can as they prepare for the "Neighbors Night Out" event. Encourage families to prepare for the event together and to use the time to get to know one another better.

On the evening of the event, have families arrive about an hour early to set up and prepare for the neighbors' arrival. As neighbors arrive, have families greet them and welcome their children to the event. Make sure parents understand what you'll be doing with their kids during the evening, and when you expect the parents to return to pick up their children. When all the neighborhood families have arrived, begin the festivities.

What Did You Think?

After the event, take some time to discuss these questions with your family:
• *How do you feel about this event?*
• *What did you enjoy most about the evening?*
• *What did you enjoy least?*
• *Was it easy to work with your family members in planning and leading this event? Why or why not?*
• *What's one way your family could improve when it comes to situations where you need to work together?*
• *Do you enjoy serving others the way you did in this event? Why or why not?*
• *What are some other ways you'd like your family to serve others?*

During the event, encourage leaders to stay with their families and work together as they lead activities, serve food, or help out in other ways. If some of your families have small children, encourage them to join in with the neighborhood kids and enjoy the activities the families have prepared.

When the event is over and all the children have gone home, give each family a copy of the "What Did You Think?" card (p. 70). On the drive home, encourage families to discuss the questions.

A few days after the event, have the "registration" families call the neighbors who've participated and thank them for allowing their children to come to the event. Ask parents how the children responded to the event and whether it was a help to parents. Also ask for any input on how to improve similar events in the future.

Taking It Home

During the event, families will get a chance to meet some of their neighbors for the first time. Encourage families to build on those new connections by inviting their neighbors for dinner or to a future church event.

Family Food Drive

Category: Service Project

Time: 3 to 4 hours

Family Focus: Families will collect canned food from neighbors for distribution to the poor.

Supplies: For each family, you'll need a Bible and a large cardboard box. You'll also need a supply of church business cards or brochures.

As families arrive, have them sit together and read 1 John 3:16-17. After everyone has arrived, say: **Today we'll have the opportunity to read what Scripture says and immediately do what it commands. Ready? Let's do it.**

Have a volunteer read aloud 1 John 3:16-17, then have participants discuss these questions with their families:

• **What do you think it means to lay down your life for someone?**

• **Have you ever laid down your life for someone? Why or why not?**

• **Have others ever laid down their lives for you? Explain.**

• **When you see someone in need, do you immediately think about how you can meet that need? Why or why not?**

• **What can we do to help the people in our city who have material needs?**

After families have had time to answer these questions, stop the discussion and ask a volunteer to read aloud 1 John 3:18. Then say: **The Word of God is clear. Our love for people in need should be more than lip service. Our love should be expressed through action and in truth. I think we should obey this Word right now.**

Give each family a cardboard box. Then say: **Lots of families in our city can't even provide the basic necessities for their children. Your challenge right now is go to your neighborhood (or any middle-class neighborhood in the city) and go door to door collecting canned goods and other nonperishable items for the poor in our city. As you go to each house, tell them who you are, what church you are from, and why you are collecting canned goods. When your box is full, you may return here to drop it off.**

When families understand their assignment, send them off to collect canned goods and other nonperishables. As families leave, give them each a supply of church business cards or brochures, so they can prove who they are to the families they visit.

When families return, gather their boxes together and congratulate families on their willingness to meet the needs of the poor in your city. When all the boxes have been collected, ask a few families to volunteer to deliver the boxes to your local soup kitchen or community center.

Taking It Home

As a continuing effort to reach out to the poor, encourage families to set up special boxes in their homes for collecting canned goods and other items to give away. Challenge every family member to place at least one item in the box each week. Whenever the box gets full, have the family go together to deliver it to the local community center or soup kitchen.

Church Makeover With a Twist

Category: Service Project

Time: 3 to 6 hours

Family Focus: Families will work together to spruce up a neighboring church.

Supplies: You'll need access to lawn maintenance equipment, gardening tools, cleaning supplies, and other assorted tools and supplies, depending on the task. You'll also need a Bible, a large thank you card, and several pens.

This service project provides a great opportunity for families to spend time together while helping another church in the area.

Before the event, contact the pastors from a handful of churches in your area and explain that a group of families from your church would like to demonstrate God's love to the body of Christ in your community by serving them in some way. Ask pastors whether there is any yardwork or other repair work that your church could do for his or her congregation. For example, in addition to basic mowing and edging, your families could trim bushes, plant flowers, paint meeting rooms, clean facilities, haul away trash, or perform simple repairs to church equipment.

When you have acquired a list of simple "service" tasks from one of the pastors, arrange a day for families to join

Family-Friendly Advice

As families prepare to work on another church's property, stress the need for them to be careful not to damage anything as they work. Be sure they understand that, if any damage does occur, they (the families involved) will be responsible for the repairs.

Family-Friendly Advice

For this project, seek out churches that have a genuine need for the kind of help you're offering. For example, many smaller churches or churches located in the inner city often struggle to keep up with the burdens of building maintenance and repair.

Family-Friendly Advice

Be sure you approach each pastor in a spirit of genuine humility. Avoid seeming to suggest that your church wants to "do them a favor." Instead, explain to the pastors that allowing your church members to serve them will help the families in your church discover the joy of serving the way Christ commands.

together and work on that church's property. Assign each family one or more of the tasks, and ask family members to provide the supplies needed to complete it. For example, if one family is responsible for trimming the bushes, ask that family to bring hedge clippers, work gloves, and trash bags to haul away the trimmings. If another family is responsible for painting a meeting room, ask that family to provide the paint, the brushes, the drop cloth, and the other supplies needed. For more expensive jobs (such as painting), assign more than one family to the task to spread out the cost.

On the day of the project, have families meet at the designated church with supplies in hand. Ask a representative from that church to direct families to their assigned tasks. Encourage families to do their best and to leave no trace of their presence when they've finished. As families finish one task, encourage them to join in helping other families until all the tasks have been completed.

After the experience, have family members take turns signing a thank you card for the church, expressing their gratitude to church members for allowing them to serve in this way.

When the last job has been completed, gather all the families together and pray for the church and its needs. Close the prayer time by reading aloud Philippians 2:1-5. Then say: **Thank you for taking on the attitude of Christ today in serving others.**

Taking It Home

Challenge families to adopt the same Christlike attitude of service in their own neighborhoods. Encourage them to look for ways they can serve their neighbors in the coming weeks. This service may be as simple as mowing a neighbor's yard for him or her. Or perhaps families might offer to help a neighbor paint his house, or another repair her fence. This month ask families to look for practical ways to show God's love to their neighbors through serving them.

Volunteer Showcase

Category: Service Project

Time: 60 to 90 minutes

Family Focus: Families will learn about several volunteer opportunities in their community and will commit to helping with one or more.

Supplies: You'll need tables and snacks.

Several weeks before this meeting, contact all of the ministry organizations or community-service organizations that operate in your area. Try to include a variety of organizations that focus on different areas of service. For example, include organizations that work with teenagers, children, single parents, prison inmates, the elderly, the sick, and the poor. Explain to each organization that your church is holding a "volunteer showcase" and that you'd like them to participate. Ask each organization whether it's able to send a representative to your church to briefly explain what the organization does and how church volunteers may help.

When you have arranged for five or six organizations to come, contact each organization's representative and explain that he or she will have ten minutes to describe what the organization does and to explain how families can help. Tell each representative that you'll also provide a table for him or her to set up a display, provide literature, or create a sign-up sheet.

Just before the event, set up one table for each organization, allowing representatives time to set up their displays. Set up another table, and fill it with snacks.

When families have arrived, explain that you're holding a "volunteer showcase" to help them discover how they can serve others in your community. Allow families about fifteen minutes to get a snack and browse the tables, then call everyone together and ask each representative to come forward and explain what his or her organization is about and how families can help.

After all the presentations have been finished, challenge family members to take a few minutes to discuss with one another which organization they would most like to participate in. Although it isn't required that family members all choose the same organization, encourage families to try to find one organization they can all feel good about working with.

After several minutes of discussion, call families together and ask them to share with the whole group what they've discussed. Challenge each family to commit to helping at least one organization in the coming month. For example, family members might volunteer to serve together at the local soup kitchen. Or they might work together to raise funds for a local after-school club.

Close by thanking the representatives for the work they do, and for allowing your families the opportunity to join in serving your community.

Taking It Home

In the coming weeks, follow up on each family's commitment by asking family members how the work is going with their chosen organization. Encourage family members to discuss not only how their volunteer work is helping others, but also how it has positively impacted their family life.

Prisoner Birthday Wishes

Category: Service Project

Time: 30 to 45 minutes

Family Focus: Families will send encouraging birthday cards to prison inmates.

Supplies: For each family, you'll need Bibles, colored pens, several blank birthday cards, and stamps. You'll also need a list of names of prison inmates who are open to receiving mail and who have birthdays coming up.

Sometime before the activity, get a list of prison inmates who have birthdays in the coming month. You can do this in several ways:

1. On the Internet, check out www.prisonpals.com. The site contains a listing of inmates and their birthdays. All the inmates at this site are open to receiving mail, and the mailing addresses are included.

2. Search the Internet for Web sites that focus on "prison ministry" or "prisoner pen pals." Look for prison ministries that offer opportunities for volunteers to correspond with inmates.

3. Check your local white pages under "prison" or the yellow pages under "church organizations." If a prison ministry has been established in your area, contact it to ask about sending birthday cards to inmates.

When you have a sufficient list (about two to three inmates per family works well), gather a blank birthday card for each inmate, and write his or her name and address on the envelope. Set out the birthday cards and other supplies for families to use.

As families arrive, have each select two or three birthday cards and several colored pens. Before explaining the purpose of the cards, read aloud Matthew 25:31-46. Then have families discuss these questions:

• **What's the main difference between the sheep and the goats in this story?**

• **Why is it important to God for us to reach out to "the least of these"?**

• **When have you reached out to someone in need?**

• **Why did you do it?**

• **What was the result?**

family-friendly Advice

If some families would like to invite their inmates to respond to their letters, encourage them to use the church's mailing address or a local P.O. Box.

After a few minutes of discussion, gather families together and say: **Today you and your family will reach out to a few of the extreme outcasts in our society. On the envelopes you're holding, I've listed the names and addresses of prison inmates who have birthdays this month. I want you and your family to work together to send an encouraging message of hope to these men and women who are behind bars.**

To complete their cards, have families follow these steps:

1. Invite family members to discuss these questions:

Family-Friendly Advice

If some families feel uncomfortable contacting prison inmates, calm their fears by encouraging them not to include a return address on their cards and to use only their first names in their letters.

• How do you think it feels to be locked away in prison?

• What do you think these prisoners need most on their birthdays?

• What can we as a family offer these inmates to bring hope to their lives?

2. Invite family members to look up encouraging Scriptures to include in the cards. After selecting one or two favorites, have someone with nice handwriting write out the verses on the backs of the birthday cards.

3. Have family members work together to compose a birthday message for each inmate. Family members may choose to write separate "little notes" in each card, or they may opt to write one message from the whole family and then have each person sign it. Either way, encourage families to be bold and compassionate in their letters, focusing on sharing the hope of Christ with each inmate.

When families have finished creating their cards, invite several volunteers to share what they've written with the whole group. Then have families seal their cards and stack them together in a pile in the center of the room. Invite families to gather around the pile, and then lead a time of prayer for the prisoners, asking God to reveal his love to them on their birthdays.

Taking It Home

Challenge families to continue praying for their inmates in the coming weeks. Encourage them to consider establishing a regular "pen pal" relationship with one or more inmates who are interested in receiving mail from new people.

Multiple-Family Rummage Sale

Category: Service Project

Time: 1 day

Family Focus: Families will plan and conduct a multiple-family rummage sale to raise money for charity.

Supplies: You'll need items for a large rummage sale and a Bible.

Several weeks before this event, tell families that you're planning a churchwide rummage sale. Explain that the rummage sale will be conducted in the church parking lot and all the proceeds will go to charity. Ask families to volunteer to help set up and run the rummage sale.

In addition, encourage family members to work together to gather items that the family no longer needs or uses. Have families price the items, then deliver them to the church.

As families prepare for this sale, invite them to suggest which charities they'd like to see benefit from the proceeds. Work with families to choose one or two organizations to receive this donation. Also determine where unsold items will be donated. Then hold the sale.

Encourage families to enjoy their time together during the rummage sale. Share the responsibilities of setting up, selling, and cleaning up, so everyone is included. Be sure to offer refreshments and a relaxed, happy atmosphere.

After the sale, deliver unsold items and the financial receipts to your designated charities.

When everything has been put away, gather families together and read 1 Timothy 6:6-10. Then discuss these questions with the whole group:

• **How did it feel to know you wouldn't be getting the money from the sale of your belongings?**

• **How does it feel knowing others will benefit from our sale?**

• **What kind of "riches" do you think serving God brings?**

• **What are other ways our families can serve God with our resources?**

Have each person think of one belonging they've donated to the rummage sale. Then have family members take turns praying that God will use those items in a special way to show God's love to others.

Taking It Home

Challenge families to keep the giving spirit alive by regularly "cleaning house" and donating unused items to local charities that need them.

Portions of this activity were adapted from an activity titled "Family Business," in 52 Fun Family Devotions (Augsburg) by Mike and Amy Nappa.

Relationship Builders

Affirmation Banners

Category: Relationship Builder

Time: 60 to 90 minutes

Family Focus: Family members will create banners to affirm one another's strengths.

Supplies: For each family, you'll need heavy butcher paper, scissors, markers (that will not bleed through the paper), masking tape, envelopes, and several of the following household items—toilet paper, a paper plate, a spatula, a pot holder, a sponge, soap, a rubber band, and a cup.

Have individual families sit in a circle. Have each family pile the household items in the center of its circle. Ask each family member to choose an item from the pile, beginning with the person who got up first this morning, then continue counterclockwise around the circle.

Allow two minutes for family members to think of all the "selling strengths" of their items. For example, someone might write that one selling strength of a paper plate is that it's better than holding your food in your hands. Then have family members take turns "pitching" their products to their family in the style of a television commercial. After all have had a chance to pitch their products, have families discuss the following questions:

Family-Friendly Advice

If you can't find enough household items or aren't confident your families will remember to bring them, have someone draw each item on a separate sheet of paper. Then photocopy each drawing for each family.

• What was it like to think of all the good things about your item?

• Would it be easier to think of all the negative aspects of your item? Why or why not?

• Is it generally easier for you to see the positive qualities in others or the negative ones? Why?

• What kind of things could each of us do to affirm one another more regularly?

After the discussion, say: **None of us affirms others as much or as often as we should. So we're going to stretch our "affirmation muscles" today by creating "Affirmation Banners" for one another.**

Set out the butcher paper, and have each person use scissors to cut a banner-sized section of the paper (about 1x4 feet works fine). Using markers, have family members divide their banners into four equal sections. Have participants write each of these headings on a different section of their paper: "Personality Strengths," "Spiritual Strengths," "Skills and Abilities," and "Relational Strengths."

Explain that participants have just drawn their own "Affirmation Banners." Have participants help one another to tape each banner to the back of the person who drew it (it's OK if some of the banners drag on the floor). Then have family members circulate around their own family, writing words of affirmation on one another's banner. For example, under "Personality Strengths," one may write, "not easily angered" or "honest." Under "Relational Strengths," one may write, "good listener" or "gives time freely."

When finished, have everyone read his or her banner. Then have family members discuss the following questions in their circles:

• **How did it feel to read what family members wrote about you?**

• **Of all the things written on your banner, which statement do you find most encouraging? Why?**

• **How did it feel to write words of affirmation for your family members?**

• **How was this experience similar to the way your family normally communicates? Why?**

• **What should you change in your family to become more affirming of one another?**

After the discussion, let family groups know that they've already taken a step toward better affirmation skills by taking part in the "Affirmation Banner" activity. Then say: **Now you'll have the opportunity to take yet another step by offering a prayer of thanksgiving for each family member's strengths.**

For this prayer time, have family members take turns kneeling in the center of their family group. Then have other family members take turns thanking God for the strengths of the family member kneeling in the center. Repeat this process until everyone has been in the center.

Taking It Home

Give family members each an envelope to decorate and tape to their bedroom doors. Encourage family members to drop affirmation notes to one another in the envelopes throughout the coming week. For example, they might say thanks for something the person did or write about a particular quality they appreciate about the person.

A Year in the Life

Category: Relationship Builder

Time: 60 to 90 minutes

Family Focus: Families will assemble "A Year of Family Life" scrapbook to preserve special events in each family's life.

Supplies: You'll need Bibles, paper, scissors, glue, tape, construction paper, and markers. You'll also need to ask each family to bring an unused scrapbook and a collection of family mementos from the past year.

In preparation for this activity, ask families to go on a "treasure hunt" through their homes looking for mementos of their lives from the past year. Children may look for certificates of class promotion or ribbons and other awards from special events. Adults may look for photographs of major events (such as birthdays and vacations), cards or notes from friends and relatives, specific Bible passages that have impacted them, or even photocopies of book covers or CDs that were especially meaningful to them during the year. Encourage all the family members to do this on their own (if possible) and not to reveal which mementos they've collected until the night of the event.

When families have arrived at the event, have each family sit together and set out its scrapbook and mementos. Then say: **The Bible places high value on a good name. Check out Proverbs 22:1, and read it together with your family. Then use the supplies I've provided to decorate the front of your scrapbook with your family name and all the names of your family members. Also be sure to include the year somewhere on the first page of the scrapbook.**

When families have finished, have them work together to compile their family scrapbooks for the previous year. Allow families to create their scrapbooks in any way they wish, making sure to include each person's memories and mementos. In addition to a chronological record of events and special memories, you might suggest that families add one or more of the following special pages to their scrapbooks: a "Where Was God?" page—ask each person to write a brief description of the role God played in his or her life past year; a "Family Answers to Prayer" page—have each family member writes a short list of personal prayers that God has answered; or a "Weirdest Experience" page—ask each family member to write about his or her strangest experience in the past year. You may add any other special page ideas you'd like.

After allowing time for each family to assemble its "A Year of Family Life" scrapbook, have each family share its scrapbook with one other family in the room. Then have the two families pray for each other, thanking God for each person in that family and asking for his guidance in the coming year.

Taking It Home

Encourage families to keep their scrapbooks available in their living or family rooms so they can add to them as new happenings occur. Then, every year, encourage families to create new "A Year of Family Life" scrapbooks to record each person's experiences.

Character Search

Category: Relationship Builder

Time: 1 to 2 hours

Family Focus: Family members will use objects they find in their homes to help them describe other members of their family.

Supplies: You'll need Bibles, construction paper, crayons, and pens.

Have family members sit together in a circle of chairs. Direct them to talk about different objects in their homes and describe the purpose for each object. For example, a microwave is used to cook things or heat things up; a television is used to entertain or provide information, and so on. Walk around the room and listen to the different things families talk about, and give them ideas if they aren't coming up with any.

After several minutes, say: **It's amazing how many different things we have in our homes. And everything has a purpose and certain characteristics. A remote control from your television set has certain characteristics and functions. It sure would be tough to try to open the garage door with it. Well, today we're going to talk about the different characteristics and functions we have as family members and how we can appreciate those in each person.**

Set out the supplies, and ask each person to take a piece of construction paper, some crayons, and a pen. Have several extra Bibles for those family members who don't have their own.

When families have their supplies, ask family members to read Psalms 1:1-3 together. Then have families discuss these questions:

• **Why do you think this person is compared to a tree?**

• **What characteristics of the tree were compared to a person who delights in the Lord?**

• **Why did the psalmist use a tree to describe the person?**

After the discussion, say: **Think about each member of your family.**

Remember when we were talking about things in our homes? Well, I want you to secretly decide which object in your house reminds you of the person on your right. Say nothing to your family now, but be prepared to explain your choice.

After a few minutes, ask each family member to draw the chosen object on one side of his or her construction paper and to draw the family member on the other side. When they've completed their pictures, have family members share with the rest of the family which object they've chosen and why they chose it. Then have each family member answer these four questions about his or her object:

- **What does that object do?**
- **Why does that object remind you of your family member?**
- **How does the object affect your family?**
- **Is that the same as the way your family member affects your family? Why or why not?**

After several minutes, have family members exchange pictures and answer this question:

- **Why do you think the other person chose that object?**

After all the groups have completed sharing, ask them to read Ephesians 4:1-5 together, then discuss these questions:

- **What words did Paul use to describe what kind of life we should live?**
- **Why is it tough to "keep the unity of the Spirit through the bond of peace" in a family?**
- **How can we extend grace to one another in our families?**

After family members have spent ample time discussing, regain everyone's attention and say: **As we work together to bring gentleness, patience, and peace to our families, God has given each of us different talents and characteristics to help us do that. Just as the objects we used to describe one another have different jobs, so do we. We should encourage one another in what we can do. As you look at your pictures, think about how you can work together as different people and encourage one another along the way.**

Encourage family members to discuss ways they can encourage one another and can help one another live together in peace.

Taking It Home

Suggest that families do this activity together at home. Have them choose several objects in their homes that represent certain characteristics about other family members. Have members explain how these items illustrate humor, work habits, sportsmanship, or other qualities that impact life within the family. Families may use this discussion to help them understand and relate to one another more effectively.

Faithopoly

Category: Relationship Builder

Time: 60 to 90 minutes

Family Focus: Family members will share personal faith experiences and tell about how God has influenced them.

Supplies: For each family, you'll need an enlarged copy of the "Faithopoly" game board (p. 89), a single die, and coins to be used as game pieces.

Before participants arrive, lay out all the supplies on a table.

As families arrive, ask them to sit together. When everyone is seated, say: **We are going to play a board game, kind of like Monopoly with a twist. I'd like each group to send one member up to the table to get your game board and die.**

When every group has a board, say: **We're going to play Faithopoly. If you look at your board, you'll see that each section on the game board asks you to share something about faith. We've provided the game boards and dice. You'll need to supply coins for your game pieces.** Give participants time to find their coins. Offer your coins to any group that comes up short.

When groups are ready, say: **To begin, each person will roll the die. The person with the highest number will go first. Simply move your piece the** number of spaces you roll, and do what it says on the space where you land. The only other rule for Faithopoly is that you get one pass in each game. That means you get to select another member of the family to do what it says on your space. Remember, you may pass only once during the game. The game is over when everyone has reached the "home" space. Ready? Go!

You may allow as much time for the game as you wish. If you're on a tight schedule, you may end the game before all families have finished. When families have concluded the game, read Deuteronomy 11:18-21, then have families discuss these questions:

• How did you feel as you played this game? Explain.

• What did you learn about someone in your family that you didn't know before?

• Why is it important for us to talk about faith as a family and with one another as Christians?

After the discussion, close with prayer.

....

Taking It Home

Allow each family to take home its game board and die. Encourage family members to find time together in the coming week to play the game again, by making up a new board with new questions that focus on a different topic of interest—for example, family history or current issues.

....

Family Builders

Category: Relationship Builder

Time: 60 to 90 minutes

Family Focus: Families will use clay models to describe their family relationships.

Supplies: For each person, you'll need a fist-sized ball of modeling clay and a sheet of wax paper. For each family, you'll need Bibles, an index card, and a pen. You'll also need a pack of gum.

Faithopoly

CHURCH

WHICH BIBLE CHARACTER IS THE BEST EXAMPLE OF FAITH TO YOU? WHY?

SHARE HOW YOUR FAITH AFFECTS YOU AT WORK OR SCHOOL.

WHEN DO YOU FEEL CLOSEST TO GOD? (MOVE AHEAD 3 SPACES)

WHO PROVIDED ONE OF YOUR EARLIEST EXAMPLES OF FAITHFULNESS?

WHAT'S THE MOST AMAZING FAITH STORY YOU'VE EVER HEARD?

TELL WHAT MAKES IT DIFFICULT FOR YOU TO TALK ABOUT YOUR FAITH.

SHARE ABOUT A DIFFICULT TIME YOUR FAITH PULLED YOU THROUGH.

(MOVE AHEAD 2 SPACES)

WHEN DO YOU FEEL FARTHEST FROM GOD?

(MOVE BACK 2 SPACES)

SHARE ONE THING YOU CAN DO TO STRENGTHEN YOUR FAITH.

WHAT'S YOUR FAVORITE WAY TO WORSHIP GOD?

TELL ABOUT SOMEONE YOU CAN TALK COMFORTABLY TO ABOUT YOUR FAITH.

TELL ABOUT SOMEONE WHOSE FAITH YOU ADMIRE AND WHY.

SHARE A TIME YOU STRUGGLED WITH YOUR FAITH.

(GO BACK 3 SPACES)

SHARE A TIME YOUR FAITH GAVE YOU GREAT JOY.

HOME

As people arrive, have them sit with their family around tables. When everyone has arrived, give each person a fist-sized ball of modeling clay and a sheet of wax paper. Tell family members to use the wax paper to protect the table surface from the clay.

Explain that you will call out a scene, and families will race to see which family can most quickly sculpt the scene. Say: **Every family member must participate, and every person's clay must be used to create the scene. Now, here's the catch—you may not talk during this activity. The only way you may communicate is through hand gestures and facial expressions. When you think your family has successfully sculpted the scene I've called out, I want you to stand up as a family and yell, "Ta Da!" so that we'll know you've finished. I'll be the judge as to whether your sculpture is accurate enough to be accepted. The first family to complete its sculpture successfully will win this pack of gum. Ready? Let's do it.**

When all the families appear ready, say: **The scene is "A family sitting around the dinner table." Begin sculpting now!**

When several families have completed their sculptures, stop the action and congratulate all the families on their creativity. Give the pack of gum to the winning family, then have families discuss these questions:

• **Did you enjoy this contest? Why or why not?**

• **What was frustrating about this activity?**

• **How is working together in silence like trying to build a strong family without really ever talking to one another?**

After the discussion, say: **Strong families are built on strong relationships. You might think the relationships in your family are already strong, but today we'll find out what other people in your family think about your family relationships. And we'll use simple clay to do it. Let me tell you how.**

Have family members each shape their clay into separate figurines that represent each of their family members. Then have family members arrange and position their figurines to represent how they view the condition of each of their family relationships. For example, if someone feels out of touch with a father but close to a sister, he or she might position the father far away with his back turned while showing the sister close by, holding the sculptor's hand. Allow families several minutes to complete their sculptures.

When family members have finished, have them take turns explaining their sculptures to their families. Then have families discuss these questions:

- **What surprises you about your family's sculptures?**
- **Which sculpture(s) shows a problem that you were unaware of?**
- **Who has the strongest relationship in your family?**
- **What makes that relationship strong?**
- **According to the sculptures, which relationship seems to be the weakest in your family?**
- **What can you do as a family to strengthen that relationship?**

After the discussion, have families read Ephesians 5:22–6:4. Based on the passage, encourage families to come up with one or two practical ways they can work together to strengthen their family relationships. Have families write their responses on an index card.

Next, have family members each reposition their clay figurines to represent the kind of family relationships they want to have with each member of the family. For example, if someone wants to be closer to Dad but is comfortable with his or her relationship with Sis, then he or she could move the dad figurine closer to his or her own, but leave the sister's figurine where it is.

When all the family members have rearranged their figurines, have families discuss these questions:

- **Based on everyone's sculpture, does it seem as though we all want the same depth of family relationship? Why or why not?**
- **What can your family members do to strengthen your relationship with each of them?**

After the discussion, have families combine all of their clay figurines to form one big heart shape. Then have families pray for God to guide each of their hearts toward building stronger relationships with one another.

Taking It Home

Have families take their index cards home. Encourage family members to get together sometime during the coming week to decide which item on the index card they're willing to try this week. When they get together, challenge families to discuss other ways they can strengthen their relationships in the coming weeks.

Big Bad Blades

Category: Relationship Builder

Time: 2 to 3 hours

Family Focus: Families will learn to rollerblade together and will participate in several fun in-line skating events.

Supplies: You'll need a large outdoor area with pavement or asphalt. You'll also need several orange cones (or some other type of boundary marker) and a first-aid kit (just in case).

For this event, have families bring from home (or rent) a pair of in-line skates for each family member. Encourage families to also bring wrist guards, kneepads, elbow pads, and a helmet for each person. If possible, contact a local in-line skating store and tell them your plans for this event. The store may be able to provide "demo" equipment for free (or rental equipment at a reduced rate) and may even provide an instructor to teach family members the proper way to rollerblade.

Ask several people who know how to rollerblade to act as "coaches" for groups of families. You'll need one coach for every six to ten people. Tell the coaches that their goal is to help family members learn the basics of skating, which includes skating forward, turning to the right or left, and stopping.

When families have arrived, form groups of six to ten and assign a coach to each group. Try to keep families together in one group. Have the coaches teach family members how to rollerblade.

After about forty-five minutes, call groups together and guide them through each of the following fun in-line skating activities. Encourage coaches to act as "spotters" in each event—working to keep anyone from falling or getting hurt.

Family Follow the Leader

On their skates, have families play Follow the Leader along a predetermined path or obstacle course. As they go along the course, have families sing a song together or recite a Bible verse together (such as John 3:16). Also, let kids lead their family around wherever they want to go.

Family Roller Hockey

Have families form teams and play roller hockey together. Use plastic foam bats and a plastic foam ball instead of hockey sticks and a puck.

Family Moving Portraits

Using an instant-print camera, have a volunteer take pictures of each family as it strikes a pose together while skating across the parking lot. Give awards for Most Impressive Shot, Scariest Shot, and Most Ridiculous Pose Ever.

When everyone seems worn out from the blading events, invite family members to a closing "pizza pigout" in which you have pizza and drinks delivered to the church for everyone to enjoy. If necessary, have families split the tab for the meal.

Taking It Home

Encourage families to go on an in-line skating tour next week, and make it a weekly practice for the next several weeks.

Lifesavers

Category: Relationship Builder

Time: 60 to 90 minutes

Family Focus: Family members will learn how they can be "lifesavers" for one another.

Supplies: For each family, you'll need Bibles, a pack of LifeSavers candy, and materials to make a mini–life preserver: cardboard, heavy white paper, blue construction paper, markers, scissors, glue, and string or small rope. You'll also need a real, round life preserver.

J ust before families arrive, hang the life preserver around your neck. Greet families as they arrive, and ask them to sit together in family groups. Give each family a package of LifeSavers candies, and have them enjoy the candy while they discuss these questions:

- Have you ever been frightened or felt as if you were in danger? Explain.
- How did you get out of danger?
- Have you ever helped someone who was afraid or was in some kind of physical danger? Explain.
- How would you feel if you knew you had literally saved someone's life?

While families talk, take the life preserver from around your neck and hang it from a prominent location in the room. After families have discussed the last question, get everyone's attention and say: **To know that you've saved someone's life would be quite a thrill, wouldn't it? Well, today we're going to learn how we can do just that. We're going to learn how we can be "lifesavers" for our families and friends. To do that, each family will create its own unique kind of lifesaver.**

Give each family supplies to create a mini–life preserver. Tell families to use the cardboard to create a lifesaver shape, then cover it in blue and white paper. Finally, have families tie the string or rope around the life preserver to create a "line."

When families have finished the lifesavers, have them discuss these questions:

- **What do you imagine it would feel like to be on a ship that's sinking in the ocean?**
- **When do you feel as if you're "sinking" in life?**
- **In those times, what would be the best way for your family to "throw you a line"?**
- **What sorts of qualities would a friend have to possess before you'd be willing to call him or her a "lifesaver" in your life?**
- **What are specific ways you could develop those same qualities in your relationships at home?**

After several minutes of discussion, break into the action and say: **Now that you have some ideas in mind, I'd like you to work together with your family to personalize your family's life preserver. Using the markers I've provided, write on your life preserver a description of the kind of lifesaver you'd want to have in your family.**

When families have finished, gather everyone together and have families share what they've written on their life preservers. Say: **We can all be lifesavers—and there's no better place to start than in our own families. Let's close by praying for one another, asking God to help us be true lifesavers for the people we love.**

Have everyone form a circle (like a life preserver) and hold hands. Close with a time of prayer, allowing time for anyone who wants to pray aloud.

Taking It Home

Tell families to take their life preservers home and hang them where everyone will see them. Challenge each family to take time each week during the next month to meet together and discuss how each member can become a better "lifesaver" for the rest of the family.

Family Feeling Discovery

Category: Relationship Builder

Time: 60 to 90 minutes

Family Focus: Family members will discover how to share their feelings by drawing pictures for one another.

Supplies: For each family, you'll need Bibles, a magnifying glass, paper, pens or pencils, a Bible concordance, and a table to work on. You'll also need one table for miscellaneous objects—such as rocks, sand, salt, a postage stamp, a dollar bill, a book, and so on.

In this activity, families will discover several things about one another. To get them into the "discovery" mode, give each family a magnifying glass and have family members take turns looking at the objects you've laid out on the table. Encourage families to point out any interesting discoveries that they would normally overlook.

Next, have families take their magnifying glasses outside for a "discovery walk" around the building. Have families look for interesting things they typically might overlook. (If weather doesn't permit, have them do the discovery walk inside.) As they go, ask them to make a list of all the things they "discover." When families have returned, ask:

• **What exciting things did you discover?**

Allow families to share their discoveries with the whole group. Then say: **Sometimes we can make great discoveries about the world around us just by taking a closer look. That same idea applies to our families. We can make great discoveries about one another—if we're willing to take a closer look. Let's take a closer look at one another right now.**

Have family members take turns using the magnifying glass to look at one another's hands and eyes. After the experience, have families discuss these questions:

• **How did it feel to be scrutinized under the magnifying glass?**

• **How is that similar to how it feels to share your deepest feelings with your family?**

• **Is it important to share feelings with your family? Why or why not?**

After the discussion, say: **Even though it can be hard, sharing our feelings with family members is important. Revealing our feelings helps our families understand us better and can deepen all of our family relationships. Today we'll use a creative idea to share our feelings with one another.**

Distribute paper, pens, and pencils and have families gather around the tables. On their paper, have family members each create a picture of how they feel at this moment. For example, they could create a picture that illustrates feeling happy, sad, confused, or angry. When they've finished the pictures, have family members take turns explaining their pictures to one another.

family-friendly Advice

If necessary, give a brief explanation of how to use a concordance. Have each family look up a word (such as "faith") and find a reference for it in the Bible. Then have families look up that verse in the Bible and read it together as a family.

As each member of the family shares, encourage family members to work together to find Scriptures that encourage someone who feels the way the picture describes. For example, if someone feels discouraged, families might look up and read Philippians 4:13 to encourage that person. Provide Bible concordances to help families find verses that apply to each family member.

When all the family members have shared, say: **Drawing pictures and sharing Scriptures is a good way to find** out how each family member is feeling, as well as a great way to apply Scriptures to life experiences.

To close your time together, have family members pray for the person on their right, praying specifically for what that person shared and thanking God for having that person in the family.

Taking It Home

Challenge families to use this activity in their worship time at home this week.

Fun With Family Photos

Category: Relationship Builder

Time: 40 to 60 minutes

Family Focus: Families will get to know one another by using family photographs to create crazy stories.

Supplies: You'll need five to eight family photographs for each family member (the wackier the better).

Before the activity, tell families to bring an assortment of family photographs—up to eight photographs per family member.

As participants arrive, have individual families form groups around tables. Then have each family exchange its photographs with one other family in the room. Be sure families don't explain the background of any of the photographs.

When families have received a stack of photos from another family, give families these instructions: Use the photos you've received to create a wild, wild story about your neighboring family. The story must have a beginning, a middle, and an ending. The more outlandish the story, the better. For example, perhaps your assigned family is secretly connected to the Mafia. Or perhaps they're aliens. Keep the story positive and affirming.

After explaining the instructions, have family members work together to create a crazy story based on the photos they've received. Tell families they don't have to use all the photographs, just enough of them to create a complete story. When families are ready, have them take turns using the photos to tell their stories to the rest of the group. As they tell their stories, encourage families to explain what's in each photograph and how it relates to the story they're telling. After each story, have families offer a round of applause.

When all the stories have been told, have families who exchanged pictures gather together in groups. Then have each person in the group select one of his or her favorite family photographs and tell the true story behind it.

After everyone has shared, have the two families join hands together and pray for each other, thanking God for the unique stories every family has to share.

Taking It Home

Now that each family has come to know one other family a little better, encourage families to continue this discovery time over dinner together. Have family groups set up a time to share a meal. At that meal, encourage family members to bring out more photographs, so they can get to know one another even better.

Memory Lane Game

Category: Relationship Builder

Time: 1 to 2 hours

Family Focus: Families will share favorite memories and express thanks for one another.

Supplies: For each family, you'll need a penny and copies of the "Memory Lane Game" (p. 100).

When everyone has arrived, give each family a copy of the "Memory Lane Game" (p. 100) and a penny. Tell families that each person will need a small coin-size object to use as a playing piece. To play, have each family follow the instructions on the game board. Tell families that the object of the game isn't necessarily to finish first, but to provide family members an opportunity to tell their "stories" and to share some of the memories that have been most meaningful to them.

Allow families to play the game for up to sixty minutes. Then have family members discuss the following questions:

• **How did it feel to share your memories?**

• **What memory did you most enjoy sharing? Explain.**

• **What memory was most difficult to share? Explain.**

• **Why do you feel it's important for us to share with one another our favorite memories?**

After the discussion, have three different family members each read aloud one of the following passages: Philippians 1:3; Philippians 4:8; and 1 Thessalonians 1:2-3. After each verse has been read, ask:

• **How does this verse apply to a person's view of the past?**

Finally, after everyone has responded, have each family member share one memory of a time another family member did something special for him or her, and why it was meaningful.

Close by having family members each say a one-sentence thank you prayer for each family member.

....

Taking It Home

Challenge families to take this game into the real world by going on a drive around town and having family members recall things they've done together at various locations. If they can, have family members recall something another family member said or did that was particularly meaningful and why. Using memories in this way can help your families strengthen their relationships and remember the good times they've had.

....

Memory Lane Game

How to play: *Start with the person who has the shortest hair, then go around to the right. When it's your turn, flip the penny. If it's heads, move your playing piece forward two spaces. If it's tails, move your playing piece forward one space. Then answer the question in the space.*

Note: *Each person has the right to "pass" on a question once during the game.*

START

What's the craziest thing you've ever done?

What's the meanest thing you've ever done?

Tell about a time you were really bored.

What's one thing you most enjoy doing with the family?

Share your favorite dating memory.

Share your saddest memory.

What's your favorite memory with a parent?

What's your favorite memory with a grandparent?

Share your favorite memory ever.

What was the most difficult thing you've ever done?

Tell about a time you were particularly proud of yourself.

Tell about the time you were most afraid.

What's the dumbest thing that has ever happened to you?

What one thing in your past would you change if you could?

Share your most embarrassing moment.

Tell about your favorite time with a brother or sister.

FINISH

Eggs-traordinary Family Fun

Category: Relationship Builder

Time: 1 to 2 hours

Family Focus: Family members will engage in several fun activities involving eggs while learning that, like the egg, each person is unique and filled with potential for growth and development.

Supplies: You'll need several dozen eggs, blindfolds, clear plastic cups, and plastic tarps.

You'll need a large room (at least 20x20 feet), preferably one with a high ceiling. Or you could consider having family members play all the egg games outside.

When families arrive, have them join with other families to form teams of about eight to ten people. Tell teams they'll play a series of games that involve eggs. To begin, choose three or more of the following games.

Egg Pass

Have teams each form separate lines, with members standing side by side. Have participants clasp their hands behind their necks and extend their elbows out in front of them. Place an egg between the elbows of the first person in each line. At your signal, have the first person in each line turn to the next person and pass the egg to him or her—using only elbows. That person then passes the egg on down the line, with each person using only his or her elbows. If any teams drop the egg, they

> ### Family-Friendly Advice
>
> *If you don't want to use real eggs, you can substitute plastic eggs filled with flour.*

must start over. The winning team is the one that passes the egg down the line first, or the team that passes the egg farthest down the line.

Egg Toss

Have team members pair up and play an old-fashioned game of egg toss. To play, have all participants stand in two parallel lines with partners standing three feet apart, facing each other. Give one partner in each pair an egg. Have this person gently toss the egg underhanded to his or her partner. If the partner catches the egg, have him or her take one step back, then toss the egg back to the first partner. Whenever anyone fails to catch the egg, both players are out of the game. The winning pair is the one that can toss the egg the farthest distance without breaking it.

Egg-Drop Scoop

Have team members pair up. Have one partner in each pair lie on the ground with eyes closed (for safety) while holding a clear plastic cup on his or her forehead. Give the other partner an egg. Tell the partner with the egg to stand above his or her teammate, crack the egg with his or her thumb, and attempt to drop its contents into the cup on the partner's forehead—all while holding the egg at eye level and at least two feet away from his or her own body. Tell pairs they each get three tries. The winning team is the one with the highest number of eggs that ended up in cups.

Nose Egg Rolling Relay

Give each team two eggs, and have teams form parallel lines, with one person behind the other. On "go," have the first person in each line get down on all fours and, using only his or her nose, roll both eggs all the way around his or her group. In turn, have each person follow suit until all members have rolled the eggs. The first team to have all its members complete the circuit wins. If any team's egg breaks during play, that team is disqualified.

Egg Gantlet

Have each team select three people to be blindfolded and to walk the gantlet in turn. (More can play if time allows.) Place several dozen eggs in an open area approximately 4x20 feet. Have teams start by blindfolding one person and having him or her walk the gantlet barefoot. Those walking the gantlet may be led only by verbal directions from their teammates. If the player bumps or breaks an egg, he or she must start the gantlet again. Play until all teams have run all three people through the gantlet. The first team to have all three of its members successfully run the gantlet wins.

After the games are over, congratulate the winning team. Then have family members join together to discuss these questions:

- **How did you feel as you played these games with eggs?**

• Why are eggs hard to handle in games like these?

• How would you describe yourself in "egg terms"? For example, are you raw, fresh, sunny side up, scrambled, fried, over easy, or hard-boiled? Explain.

• How is our human potential for growth and change like an egg?

• How do our human potential "eggs" get broken?

Gather families together, and have a volunteer read aloud Psalm 139:13-16. Then lead this short discussion:

• What encouraging truth do you think God would want us to pull from this passage?

• How do you think each of us can help one another reach our potential?

• How can we help others grow stronger in ways they feel weak?

Hold up the egg. Say: **In this egg is everything necessary to become a chicken. Had this egg not been deprived of the warmth, nurture, and sacrificial efforts of its mother, it would have become a chicken that, in turn, could have produced many more chickens. But now, the best this egg can hope for is to become an omelet. Each of us can have a huge impact on whether the members of our families will realize their full potential. We can invest in one another's growth and potential through offering encouragement and affirmation, and by being willing to sacrifice for another person's good.**

Have each family form a circle, then give each family an egg. Have family members pass the egg around their circle. As each person receives the egg, have that person share one area of life in which he or she would most like to grow and develop. For example, a parent may share a desire to complete college. Or a young person may share a desire to play a particular sport or pursue a certain hobby.

Close by having family members pray individually for each person in their group according to what that person shared.

Taking It Home

Encourage families to continue this discussion by going out to dinner together and brainstorming practical ways they can encourage one another in their respective aspirations.

Mystery Meal

Category: Relationship Builder

Time: 40 to 60 minutes

Family Focus: Without knowing what the other members of their family are preparing, family members will together prepare a meal plan and so they can learn more about working together as a family.

Supplies: For each family, you'll need pencils, index cards, cookbooks, and snacks.

A s family members enter the room, have them sit together at the tables. Give each family a supply of snacks, and say: **We're going to have some fun today, so I hope everyone came with an "appetite" for laughter. As a family, you're going to create a mystery meal plan, full of foods that you like. Each of you will have a different part of the meal to plan. The fun part about your meal is that none of you will know what the rest of you are planning. Let's see what kinds of food combinations we can come up with.**

Family-Friendly Advice

To add a little spice to this lesson, you may want to wear an apron and a chef's hat. You could also use an egg timer to keep time during the discussions.

Assign each family member a different part of the mystery meal to prepare. For example, you need someone to prepare an appetizer, a main dish, a side dish, and a dessert. If a family has more than four people, have the additional family members plan appetizers or side dishes. Set out assorted cookbooks for families to use. Provide index cards and pencils, and have family members copy the recipes they've chosen onto index cards. Make sure families don't discuss their food planing choices.

When families are ready, have family members take turns sharing their plans for the mystery meal, beginning with the appetizer and going all the way through dessert. After the plan has been revealed, have families discuss these questions:

• **Do you think the meal we've planned would be good to eat? Why or why not?**

- How is planning a "mystery" meal in this way similar to what happens when we try to plan activities together as a family, such as a vacation or some other kind of family outing?

- When your family makes plans, do you ever feel as if your desires are ignored? Why or why not?

- Why is it important that every member of a family be considered when plans are made that affect everyone?

- How can we do a better job of considering everyone's needs and wishes when making family plans?

After the discussion, say: Next, we're going to continue with our food experience. Give each family more index cards, and say: I want you to go through the cookbooks and finish planning the meal you've started. For example, if you've planned an appetizer, complete the plan by adding your own favorite main dish, side dish, and dessert. Once you've chosen your dishes, copy the recipes onto index cards.

When families have finished the mean plans, have each member share with the family what he or she created. Then say: Now you have a new understanding of one another's likes and dislikes. And that's the first step in learning how to work together more effectively as a family!

To close this time, lead everyone in a closing prayer. Ask God to bless the family mealtime and to help families use it to strengthen their bonds with one another.

Taking It Home

Encourage families to prepare one family member's "favorite meal plan" each week for the next several weeks. The catch—let each family member fix his or her own special meal for the family. During the meal, have family members quiz the chef on his or her other likes and dislikes in life.

Generosity Bracelets

Category: Relationship Builder

Time: 40 to 60 minutes

Family Focus: Families will learn about generosity while creating bracelets to give away.

Supplies: For each person, you'll need Bibles, scissors, nylon line (or leatherette cord), and enough plastic beads (6 mm or 8 mm) to make a simple bracelet. For each family, you'll need paper and pencil and a list of the verses used in this activity.

Gather families around tables, and invite the members of each family to take turns completing the following statements:

- **I feel most generous when...**
- **I feel least generous when...**

Ask one person in each family to take notes on the responses and be prepared to quickly share them with the rest of the group. When families have finished, have the note takers each give a brief report to the whole group.

Say: **The Bible tells us a lot about the importance of generosity. I'll provide your family with a list of verses that encourage us toward cheerful generosity. As you read through these verses, I want each of you to talk about the role generosity should play in your family, and then create a generosity bracelet to help you remember what you've learned.**

> **Family-Friendly Advice**
>
> Hobby and craft stores will have a wide range of beads to choose from. Look for beads with holes that can be easily strung by children.

Set out supplies for each family. Provide each family with a list of the assigned Bible passages. Ask group members to take turns reading each of the following verses and explaining what each teaches about generosity in family life: Psalm 112:9; Proverbs 11:24-25; Proverbs 19:17; Jeremiah 17:7-8; Matthew 7:7-12; Luke 6:38; Acts 20:35; and 2 Corinthians 9:6-8.

After discussing each verse, have family members each string a bead onto their bracelet as a symbol of the lesson on generosity. If the group wants, it may find other Scripture passages on generosity and then string more beads.

Before everyone has finished, tell people *not* to tie their bracelets. Say: **As a way to help us practice generosity, I want to ask you to give your bracelet to another family member as a gift. Tie your bracelet around your family member's wrist. While you do this, tell the person one thing you appreciate about him or her and one practical way you're going to express generosity to that person this week. For example, you might offer to wash your father's car or fix dinner for the family one night this week.**

After everyone has shared a generosity bracelet, invite the group to form a large circle and join hands to form a giant bracelet of joy. Close your time together by singing a song or chorus on generosity and giving to others—for example, "Joyful, Joyful, We Adore Thee," or "Give Thanks."

Taking It Home

Have families take home their bracelets along with a list of all the Bible verses they've read in this activity. Invite them to take time during family worship at home to read additional verses and to add more beads to their bracelets. Also encourage family members to wear the generosity bracelets during the week as reminders of what the Bible says about remembering others.

Scavenger Scurry

Category: Relationship Builder

Time: 2 to 3 hours

Family Focus: Family members will work as a team to complete a scavenger hunt.

Supplies: For each family, you'll need plastic bags, Bibles, pencils, notepads, paper, and crayons.

When everyone has arrived, say: **How many of you have been on a scavenger hunt? Well, today we're going to go on a scavenger hunt as families.**

Give each family a bag, a pencil, and a notepad. Say: **Today's scavenger hunt has a twist. Instead of giving you a list of things to find, you're going to decide as a family which things you want to collect. I'll explain more about that in a minute. First, we'll read about a special family in the Bible.**

Turn to Genesis 6 and 7, and ask several volunteers to read the Scriptures. After the group has read both chapters, ask:

• How would you have felt in Noah's place?

• Besides the animals, what else do you think Noah and his family might have taken on the ark?

Say: **Can you imagine being the family that God chose to go on the ark? Noah must have felt both fear and honor as he accepted God's invitation.**

Now, back to our plastic bags. Let's say God speaks to you and your family and tells you he has chosen you to go on a trip. You have only a short time to gather some personal belongings. Unfortunately, each person can take only one personal item. As a family, you need to decide what you're going to take with you. Nothing is too crazy or wrong. Remember, you each get only one item, so you need to put some thought into it. After each person has decided, list the object on the notepad.

Say: **Here's your next assignment. I'll give you several minutes to go and collect your items. Place all of your objects in the plastic bag, and return to this room as soon as possible.**

Give your families as much time as possible to collect the items. For those who have to go home and don't live near the church, have them use crayons to draw their items and place their drawings in the bag.

When families have returned with their items, have each member discuss these questions:

• Why did you choose the object you did?

• What purpose will that object serve on your trip?

• Will your object be helpful to the rest of the family, or will it only be helpful to you? Explain.

After the discussion, say: **Now let's go back to Noah and his family. God chose Noah because he was a righteous man. Even so, I'm sure that while Noah and his family were building the ark, people made fun of them. Noah and his family probably became discouraged, but they remained steadfast. Why? One reason may have been that they had one another for encouragement.**

We're each on a journey through life. Just as Noah did, we each face ridicule and unforeseen dangers. When faced with such a challenge, it's easy to think primarily about ourselves. We think about the things that *we* need to survive, not the things that our family needs. But it doesn't have to be that way.

Let's turn the tables on selfish thinking. You've each chosen a personal item to take with you on your journey through life. Instead of thinking of how that item can help you, think about how it can help someone else in your family. I want you to think of ways you can encourage one another during the week by using your personal item. For example, if your personal item is a journal, you might use it to write encouraging notes to your family members. Or if your personal item is a Bible, you might share with your family specific Bible verses that are meaningful to you.

After a few minutes, give family members a chance to share with their families how they'll use their personal items to encourage one another.

After each family member has shared, have families close in prayer by holding their objects and completing this one-sentence prayer: **Dear God, I want to encourage my family this week by** [fill in the blank], **amen.**

Taking It Home

In addition to using their personal items as encouragement tools, you might suggest that families place their items someplace in their homes where they will remind everyone about the lesson. Also, encourage families to get together each night to share what they've done during the day and to discuss new ways they can encourage one another.

Family Friendliness
Fosters Friendships

Category: Relationship Builder

Time: 45 to 60 minutes

Family Focus: Family members will recognize the importance of being friendly inside and outside the family.

Supplies: For each family, you'll need paper, pencils, Bibles, and photocopies of the "Friendship Factor Quiz" (p. 112).

To begin this activity on the importance of friendliness for building friendships, challenge family members to work together to come up with ten items from their purses or wallets that remind them of their friends. Qualifying items could be a dollar a friend gave them, a picture of a friend, a note from a friend, a comb or brush like one a friend uses, or other items like these. Each family member should come up with at least one item that reminds him or her of a friend.

After families have gathered their items, have family members take turns telling their family why they chose their items, why the items remind them of their friends, and one significant memory of each friend.

After several minutes, have each family present to the whole group the most "unusual" item or connection between an item and friend. Then lead the whole group in a short discussion:

• How did you feel as you searched for items that reminded you of friends?

• When you think back to the friendships you spoke of, what qualities of friendliness or acts of kindness drew you to one another?

• In your experiences, how important is kindness when it comes to beginning and developing friendships?

Say: To make friends and build friendships, it's essential that we be friendly and kind, and take an interest in others. Let's look at a few Bible passages that show us more about the importance of friendliness in making friendships.

Distribute paper and pencils to each family. Assign one of the passages below to each family. If your group is small, it's OK to assign more than one passage to each family.

- 1 Samuel 18:1-4; 19:1-2; 20:4
- John 15:12-14 and Romans 12:10
- 1 John 4:7-12
- Mark 12:28-31

Write the following two questions on chalkboard or newsprint for families to see. On their own paper, have families work together to answer the two questions based on the passage(s) they've been assigned:

- **What does this passage say about friendship?**
- **What does this passage say about friendliness or kindness in establishing friendships?**

After several minutes, have families report their responses to the whole group. Then ask:

- **How were you most challenged by these passages and responses we've shared?**
- **What are some specific, practical expressions of friendliness that we should practice toward everyone? toward those with whom we are closest?**
- **Tell of a time in your own life when someone's practical expression of kindness endeared you to him or her.**

Say: **Let's explore our own friendliness.** Distribute the "Friendship Factor Quiz" (p. 112) to everyone. Allow two or three minutes for the group to complete this quiz. Then, in their families, have group members discuss the following questions:

- **How did you feel as you completed this quiz? Why?**
- **What did this quiz show you about you and your friendliness?**
- **How does what we have learned about friendliness apply to us within our family?**
- **What is one thing you will do to exercise more friendliness within your family? toward your friends? toward new people you meet?**

Have family member's close by praying for one another according to what each has shared.

Friendship Factor Quiz

Instructions: Rate yourself on each of the following friendliness characteristics from 1 (always true) to 5 (never true).

I don't make fun of or put down other people.	1	2	3	4	5
I am a friend to my parents.	1	2	3	4	5
I share what I have with others.	1	2	3	4	5
I treat people the way I want to be treated.	1	2	3	4	5
People welcome me into their groups.	1	2	3	4	5
Shy people seek me out.	1	2	3	4	5
When I like something about someone, I let that person know it.	1	2	3	4	5
When I am wrong, I have no trouble apologizing.	1	2	3	4	5
I'm a good listener.	1	2	3	4	5
I'm a friend to my family members.	1	2	3	4	5
I let people know that I care about them.	1	2	3	4	5
I quickly forgive people when they hurt me.	1	2	3	4	5
I stick up for my friends.	1	2	3	4	5
I accept the differences in personality, opinion, and music preferences of my friends.	1	2	3	4	5
I try not to embarrass my friends in front of other people.	1	2	3	4	5
I go out of my way to begin friendships.	1	2	3	4	5
I stand by my promises.	1	2	3	4	5
I try hard to see things from other people's point of view.	1	2	3	4	5
I try to encourage other people.	1	2	3	4	5
I brag on my friends and their achievements.	1	2	3	4	5
I'm there for my friends when they need me.	1	2	3	4	5
I do nice things for other people.	1	2	3	4	5

Taking It Home

Encourage family members to take their quizzes home and to discuss them over dinner together. Challenge family members to talk openly with one another about how they can deepen their friendships with one another. Based on their conversation, encourage family members to change one thing about the way they demonstrate kindness or friendship with other members of the family.